2021#5

NEW IN CHESS

5 Contents

'Chess players are not always great at switching conversation topic in the presence of non-chess playing company'

CONTRIBUTORS TO THIS ISSUE

Joel Benjamin, John Burke, Cristian Chirila, Anish Giri, John Henderson, Luke McShane, Abhi Mishra, Peter Heine Nielsen, Hans Niemann, Maxim Notkin, Judit Polgar, Matthew Sadler, Han Schut, Harold Scott, Sam Sh... ...lls,

T0054279

The World Champion

It's a retro 1970s Soviet chess scene that looks strangely familiar, but odd. The player with the white pieces, couldn't he vaguely pass for a young Anatoly Karpov? And standing next to him

could that be Mikhail Tal? It looks as if it's taken at the Moscow Central Chess Club, and for added authenticity there's a trusty supply of *Shakhmatny Bulletin*'s from the era. This is one of the first look images

released by the Russian film distribution and production company, Central Partnership, for their new release, *The World Champion* (with English sub-titles), a pulled-from-the headlines story based on the

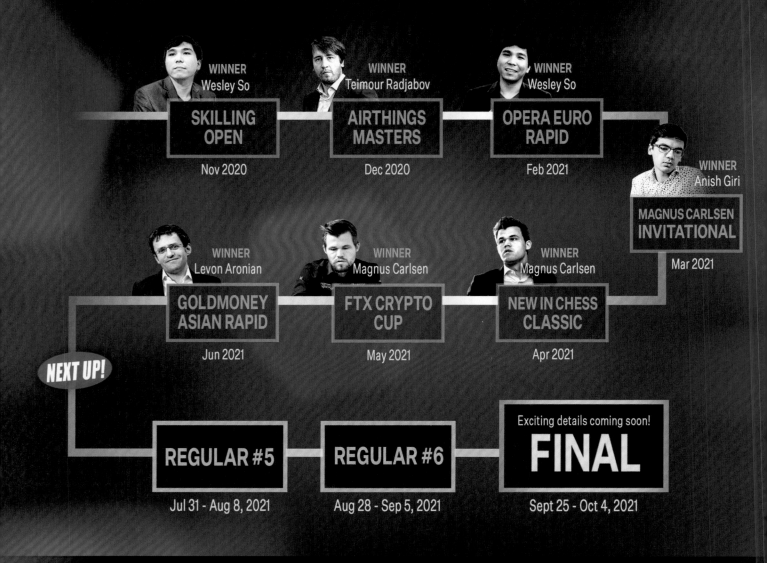

controversial 1978 World Championship Match in Baguio City between Soviet hero Anatoly Karpov and dissident Viktor Kortchnoi. *The World Champion* is written and

helmed the WWII blockbuster *T-34*, and it stars established character actor Konstantin Khabensky (Kortchnoi) and rising newcomer Ivan Yankovsky (Karpov) in the

The movie is scheduled for its theatrical release on December 30, 2021 and from there it will then go on show during the 2022 International Film Festival circuit before arriving

Messi Chess

We all know Magnus Carlsen is Real Madrid's VIP chess fan, as is his title challenger Ian Nepomniachtchi for FC Spartak Moscow. Now the latest to come to the Café's attention is Nona Gaprin-

Nona Gaprindashvili (80) proudly shows the signed Messi shirt (10).

dashvili being a long-time fan of FC Barcelona, and especially their talismanic star Lionel Messi.

In early May, on the occasion of the five-time women's ex-World Champion's 80th birthday, she received a special gift of one of Messi's No.10 Barça shirts, signed by Messi and with a personal message of 'Happy anniversary, Nona, a big greeting'.

The surprise was arranged through FIDE by vice-president Akaki Iashvili, who handed the gift over to the Georgian legend on her big day. 'It is something so unexpected and so gratifying', a surprised Gaprindashvili said. 'The shirt will occupy a place of honour in my museum, alongside my collection of chess awards and other international trophies.'

And the winner is...

It's not often we see chess being honoured in the design industry's annual shindig, but this year's European Design Awards saw the Play Magnus Group's innovative logo for the Meltwater Champions Chess Tour pick up two gold medals in the Motion Logos and Digital categories.

The eye-catching design – which features graphical representations of iconic chess games and changes for every event – was conceived by the Norwegian agency Schjærven Reklamebyrå. To create the new visual profile and identity for the Tour, project lead Helge Wiig and his creative team came up with a 3D animated logo that can be generated for any chess game and shows the drama of how it unfolds over the chessboard.

The logo has seen eight versions so far – the overall Tour logo and one for each of the seven tournaments. The 2021 season opener Skilling Open logo, for example, was generated from 13-year-old Bobby Fischer's famous 'Game of the Century' win over Donald Byrne in 1956. The Tour's overall logo was the thriller from August 2020, the closely-contested Armageddon decider

Winning in style. A Carlsen-Nakamura Armageddon classic turned logo.

between Magnus Carlsen and Hikaru Nakamura that concluded the first season's final.

The Irish Problem

When it comes to problems, Jim 'JJ' Walsh is 'yer man', as they would say in Dublin. Affectionately known to all as JJ, at the age of 89 he recently reflected on his long and distinguished 66-year career as the daily chess puzzle compiler for *The Irish Times* and on the occasion of reaching a milestone 15,000th edition in the newspaper.

His first column appeared on 7 July 1955 and was weekly. But after writing

daily reports for the newspaper during the global chess frenzy of the 1972 Fischer-Spassky match – which bought his wife Maureen a fancy new set of plush curtains – he shrewdly

Looking for problems? No problem for 89-year-old Jim 'JJ' Walsh.

managed to talk his editor into running a daily chess problem.

In his formative chess years, JJ also represented Ireland in three Olympiads in the 1950s, with his most memorable highlight being Munich '58 when he was beaten by World Champion Mikhail Botvinnik – just one of three successive opponents and defeats that also included Bent Larsen and Dr Max Euwe!

It was a fitting and wholesome tribute from the *Irish Times*, but they were being a little disingenuous in describing their man as being 'the longest-running chess columnist ever.' That accolade surely goes to Leonard Barden at *The Guardian*, with the evergreen 91-year-old writing his always topical column since April 12, 1956. A more accurate tag for JJ would be 'the longest-running chess puzzle compiler ever.'

Slumdog Billionaire

In mid-June, filled with nothing but good intentions, Vishy Anand took part in his 'Checkmate COVID fundraiser', a glitzy online simul organized on chess.com against nine celebrity opponents. The aim was to raise money for the Indian charity offering hope to those affected by the pandemic.

His star-studded field – from cricket, film, entertainment and business – included Nikhil Kamath, Yuzvendra Chahal, Kichcha Sudeep, Sajid Nadiadwala, Riteish Deshmukh, Aamir Khan, Arijit Singh, Anaya Birla, and Manu Kumar Jain. What could possibly go wrong in a big celebrity charity chess fund-raiser, especially against a legendary ex-World Champion, and it being backed by the Indian media, you might wonder?

Being caught red-handed cheating for one, it seems. Anand won eight of the nine games, but faced 'unexpected' difficulties in one and suffered his only loss to Nikhil Kamath. But many fans following the event were growing suspicious of the play of the entrepreneur – plus one or two others – especially with a 'stunning engine accuracy' that ran at 99%. Chess.com has a zero-tolerance for cheating, and his account was quickly banned, with further bans also being handed out to Sajid Nadiadwala and Kichcha Sudeep for similar offences.

And seeing which way the media and social media feeding frenzy was going, the billionaire co-founder of Zerodha was forced into a public apology on Twitter: 'In my head, it

Nikhil Kamath took his game to a whole different level.

was just a fun game we amateurs were playing against the greatest chess champ from India to raise funds for charity. But it still gives no excuse for what I did. It was wrong, and I sincerely apologise.'

Enigma Variation

It seems in Spain there's a new super hero pounding the streets of Madrid, and he looks a little bit like a chessic version of Spiderman. But this is no comic book fictional character, as he's a real mysterious chess player known only as 'Rey Enigma', King Enigma. He suddenly pops up in public spaces to challenge anyone to a quick game.

To keep his identity a secret, he's dressed head to foot in a black and

The mysterious Rey Enigma pays 100 euros if you beat him.

white checkered jumpsuit that simulates a chessboard. His secret weapon is his chess set, board and clock, and to sweeten the prospects of playing him, this peculiar character also offers €100 to anyone who manages to beat him.

Rey Enigma has now become a popular figure in the Spanish capital, usually appearing unexpectedly in popular places, such as the Retiro or Opera, to throw down a challenge to his would-be rivals. He's also caught the attention of the media, making many appearances on TV news slots as they try to unmask our hero.

With his voice electronically disguised so as not to reveal his identity, he told one TV interviewer: 'At first I started with the idea of the Enigma King without consulting anyone. My passion since I was 5 years old was chess. I started uploading a couple of videos on TikTok and they went viral. There are many creators of very good chess

content, I had to seek and provide a differential value using my disguise.'

Apparently only a handful of people know his true identity. Several players he's played have suggested the names of various grandmasters underneath the outfit, but as yet no one has managed to beat him.

Love, Tennis & Chess

Some say that tennis is like chess. That's why we were intrigued to see this photo appear during a rain-break at Wimbledon, which revealed just what the fabled green-outfitted young court staff get up to during their enforced downtime: they organize an impromptu 'winner-stays-on' chess challenge!

There's many top chess stars who play tennis. Bobby Fischer and Boris Spassky played, as did Lubosh Kavalek and Ulf Andersson. And every year, the TC RW Baden-Baden, one of Germany's top tennis clubs, in conjunction with the Bundesliga Baden-Baden Chess Club, organises a combined chess/tennis tournament. In 2018 they staged the first-ever Chess Tennis World Championship, with four grandmasters taking

Even behind the scenes tennis looks like chess.

part, and Laurent Fressinet winning the title.

The next event runs 7-8 August with Fressinet defending his title against GMs Pavel Tregubov, Alexandra Kosteniuk and Sébastien Mazé. ∎

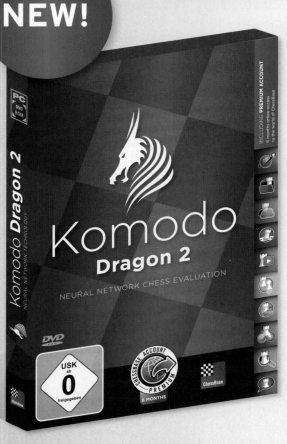

Letter of the Month

Steaks and Stakes

As always it was a pleasure to see New In Chess 2021/4 pop up on my iPad. However, I think the extract in the magazine from *The Unstoppable American* – Jan Timman's new book on Bobby Fischer – contains a small mistake. In both the book and the extract, Timman quotes a tripartite phone conversation between Fischer, Petrosian and Gligoric (acting as Russian-English translator) to discuss the location of the upcoming Fischer-Petrosian match, remarking in arguing for Buenos Aires that 'Fischer brought forward that the steaks in Argentina were excellent, which wasn't a strong argument in itself'.

Though this assessment is consistent with the transcript of the call contained in Frank Brady's *Profile of a Prodigy*, which I assume is Jan Timman's source, the rest of the discussion revolved around money. Hence, it seems very likely to me the stenographer's summary of Fischer stating on Buenos Aires 'they make excellent *steaks* there' is mistaken, and Fischer made reference to the stakes on offer via the prize fund, with the stenographer subsequently adjusting Fischer's phrasing to be consistent with their misunderstanding of steak. That Petrosian responded, 'For me, climate and general conditions are most important, not financial' is also consistent with Gligoric understanding Fischer to reference money and translating stakes, not steak. While Fischer was a great eater throughout his life, his primary focus in the run up to Reykjavik was almost invariably money.

Paul Heaton,
Epping, UK

Superior study

I would like to express my thanks to Jan Timman for continuing to treat us to endgame studies, as he did in his article My Favourites in New In Chess 2021/1. Is Oleg Pervakov the 'greatest' composer? That's always open for discussion. About his first prize in the Persitz Memorial 2019 that is given, I'd like to say the following: the starting position troubles me a bit, the first move with check, too. These are rather short fireworks with a beautiful final position.

However, 70 years ago V. Korolkov won a 1st prize (Lelo 1951!; no doubt to be found in Harold van der Heijden's study database) with a much more natural starting position, light like whipped cream, with a subtle division of tasks for the kings, and with the same final position as Pervakov's.

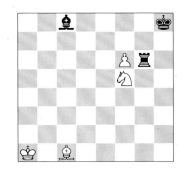

The position looks as if it was taken from a game.
White to win in 12 (instead of 6 moves).
In *Secrets of Spectacular* Chess (Batsford 1995) by J. Levitt and D. Friedgood the authors write on pages 146/147: 'If you have never seen this study before and fail to find it exciting, our only advice is to give up the game straight away. You will have no future in chess!'

Closer to our time, in Jonathan Rowson's *The Moves that Matter* (Bloomsbury 2019) this study is referred to in the chapter 'Truth and Beauty'.

The solution I will not give, as you can find it everywhere [as we are not entirely sure of that, let us give the solution anyway:
1.f7 ♖a6+ 2.♗a3! (2.♔b2 ♖f6!) 2...♖xa3+ 3.♔b2 ♖a2+ (3...♖b3+ 4.♔a2!) 4.♔c1! ♖a1+ 5.♔d2 ♖a2+ 6.♔e3 ♖a3+ 7.♔f4 ♖a4+ 8.♔g5 ♖g4+! 9.♔h6! ♖g8! (9...♖g6+ 10.♔xg6 ♗xf5+ 11.♔f6) 10.♘e7! ♗e6 11.fxg8♕+ ♗xg8 12.♘g6 mate – ed.].

Personally, I find this study superior. Levitt & Friedgood also mention a 'weaker' study (two years before the Korolkov study) by J. Selman.

Thanks again to Jan Timman for his work on studies and his analytical work.

Bernard de Bruycker
Ghent, Belgium

COLOPHON

PUBLISHER: Remmelt Otten
EDITOR-IN-CHIEF:
Dirk Jan ten Geuzendam
HONORARY EDITOR: Jan Timman
CONTRIBUTING EDITOR: Anish Giri
EDITORS: Peter Boel, René Olthof
PRODUCTION: Joop de Groot
TRANSLATOR: Piet Verhagen
SALES AND ADVERTISING: Edwin van Haastert
PHOTOS AND ILLUSTRATIONS IN THIS ISSUE:
Jeremy Bibuld, Austin Fuller, Vladimir Jagr, Lennart Ootes, John Upham Photography, Berend Vonk
COVER DESIGN: Hélène Bergmans

© No part of this magazine may be reproduced, stored in a retrieval system or transmitted in any form or by any means, recording or otherwise, without the prior permission of the publisher.

NEW IN CHESS
P.O. BOX 1093
1810 KB ALKMAAR
THE NETHERLANDS

PHONE: 00-31-(0)72-51 27 137
SUBSCRIPTIONS: nic@newinchess.com
EDITORS: editors@newinchess.com
ADVERTISING: edwin@newinchess.com

WWW.NEWINCHESS.COM

Budapest or bust

Abhi Mishra is the youngest GM ever at 12 years, 4 months and 25 days

AUSTIN FULLER

Father and son had travelled to Budapest on a mission: for young Abhi to compete in as many chess tournaments as were needed to become the youngest grandmaster in history. On June 30, the title was a fact, when Abhimanyu ('Abhi') Mishra, the preteen from Englishtown, New Jersey, shattered the previous record held since 2002 by Sergey Karjakin with 66 days to spare. **JOHN HENDERSON** spoke to Hemant and Abhi Mishra about their most remarkable adventure and the new stunning record. Abhi's next goal? To be a 2700+ Super GM before he is 15!

What makes Abhi Mishra's title chase all the more remarkable and fascinating was how it was done, in seemingly impossible circumstances during an ongoing global pandemic. The bold game-plan involved Abhi – already with many age records to his name, including the youngest ever international master at 10 years 9 months – and his father Hemant, jumping on a plane on 11 April as lockdown restrictions began to ease. They had bought two one-way air tickets to Budapest for a concentrated campaign to either break the record or bust.

Father and son were prepared for the long haul by staying in a rented apartment in the Hungarian capital, where they confined themselves as much as they could within their own bubble for safety. And once settled in, Abhi started to play non-stop in a series of back-to-back First Saturday and Vezérképzo GM tournaments, ready to continue doing so right up to the deadline date of 5 September to crack Karjakin's 19-year record. But apparently the strangeness of the situation through Covid only seemed to bring out Abhi's inner strength and gritty determination. In the end he completed the mission with the pair 'only' having to spend three months in Budapest.

'It took some determined planning in a race against time in these strange days,' explained Hemant, when I caught up with them both in Budapest on Skype from their modest little apartment. With wife Swati and daughter Ridhima safely back home in New Jersey, they were only able to follow Abhi's progress online, and the normally close family had to rely on daily reunions over Skype to stay sane through it all. Apart from missing their friends and family, Hemant also explained that, more than most, they were acutely aware of the pandemic dangers, with his own father having been lost to Covid last year.

More intense training

Originally the plan was to launch a tilt at Karjakin's record back in 2020, looking to obliterate it by as much as anything up to six months or more. But then along came Covid and the world shut down, and frustratingly their campaign had to be put on what seemed an indefinite hold. Yet this enforced time at home was put to good use. Abhi wisely avoided getting caught up in playing all the myriad of online chess tournaments. Instead he opted for more intense online chess training sessions with his coaches – GMs Arun Prasad, Mahesh Panchanathan and Pentala Harikrishna. This, they firmly believe, really helped to develop and mature his game for the coming demands.

Plus, being naturally academically gifted, the time was also used constructively with Abhi breezing his way through 5th and 6th grade studies at Seashore Day School. And so being a year ahead, this allowed for a mini-sabbatical and their Budapest odyssey. It also helped enormously

that Hemant could remotely work online, being a Senior Technical Manager with Commvault Systems, a major data protection and data management software company in New Jersey.

Abhi completed the mission with the pair 'only' having to spend three months in Budapest

But a strong and positive start in Budapest went a long way in confirming Hemant's belief that his son could break the record. Despite the pressures, the pandemic concerns and being jet-lagged, he was reassured when Abhi quickly settled at the board with a long struggle and a solid draw against the 2525-rated Czech GM Vojtech Plat. He then kept up the relentless pace with 70 games in 78 days, playing in three editions of

Abhi Mishra

2009 Born 5 February in Englishtown, New Jersey, USA
2011 Learned to play chess from his father at the age of two-and-a-half
2014 Played his first competitive rated tournament aged 5
2016 Youngest ever USCF Expert aged 7
2018 Youngest ever USCF Master aged 10
2019 World's youngest IM at 10 years and 7 months
2021 World's youngest GM at 12 years, 7 months and 25 days

both the First Saturday and the Vezér-képzo GM tournaments, winning three of them along the way.

Amazing swindle

But this isn't a story about winning tournaments, it's all about attaining norms and gaining valuable Elo-rating points. And after the adrenalin-rush of two relatively quick-fire norms and crossing the crucial 2500 barrier, the final norm wasn't coming as easy as the others did. 'I just kept missing it by a half point or so,' mused

Abhi Mishra at home with his parents and sister Ridhima. During the expedition to Budapest the family stayed in touch via Skype.

Abhi. 'I went through some bad luck, and began to think the third norm might never come. That we have to leave Budapest disappointed… and then suddenly the good luck came my way!'

That 'good luck' moment, as he describes it, was to come on Wednesday 30 June in the penultimate round of the Vezérképzo GM Mix tournament. Needing to win at all costs, and constantly over-pressing from an equal position against the young Indian GM Leon Mendonca, his position began to rapidly deteriorate. But we all need a little smile now and again from Lady Luck in chess, and with his opponent down to his last 12 seconds or so, a wrong king-move allowed Abhi to seize his chance. On the alert, he uncorked an amazing swindle worthy of an entry in the second edition of David Smerdon's award-winning *The Complete Chess Swindler*.

Leon Luke Mendonca
Abhimanyu Mishra
Budapest Vezerkepzo 2021 (9)

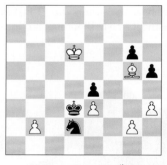

position after 47…♘d2

The tale of this crucial game is that Abhi could easily have drawn, but he needed a win for his final norm, so he's pushed the envelope to try to complicate the position – and he soon gets his reward.
48.♔e5? Down to his last few seconds, Mendonca walks right into what turns out to be an epoch-making blunder. The correct way to win was 48.b4! and use the passed b-pawn as a 'decoy'.

The 10 youngest GMs ever

			Y – M – D
1	Abhimanyu Mishra	USA	12 – 4 – 25
2	Sergey Karjakin	Ukraine	12 – 7 – 0
3	Gukesh Dommaraju	India	12 – 7 – 17
4	Javokhir Sindarov	Uzbekistan	12 – 10 – 5
5	R. Praggnanandhaa	India	12 – 10 – 13
6	Nodirbek Abdusattorov	Uzbekistan	13 – 1 – 11
7	Parimarjan Negi	India	13 – 4 – 22
8	Magnus Carlsen	Norway	13 – 4 – 27
9	Wei Yi	China	13 – 8 – 23
10	Raunak Sadhwani	India	13 – 9 – 28

48…♘f3+! After enduring some bad luck a couple of rounds earlier, losing to GM Milan Pacer from a clearly better position, now good luck comes Abhi's way with a high-class swindle that dramatically turns the game.

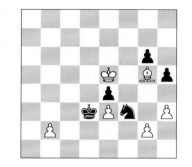

49.gxf3? Mendonca commits the fatal blunder, now allowing a study-like finish. After 49.♔f6! it's just a draw, as after 49…♘xg5 50.♔xg5 ♔xe3 51.b4! both pawns safely queen.
49…exf3 50.♗h4 g5! 51.♗f2 ♔e2

52.b4 There's no defence. After 52.♗g1 ♔f1 53.♔e4 g4! 54.hxg4 hxg4 55.♗h2 ♔g2 Black's advanced passed pawns will win.

52…♔xf2 53.b5 ♔xe3 54.b6 f2 55.b7 f1♕ And White resigned, as after 56.b8♕, 56…♕f4+ would win the queen.

And with that touch of élan, not only did young Abhi earn himself go on to earn himself clear first place with a score of 7/9, he also now enters the record books with his third norm and the youngest grandmaster in chess history. A chess record that officially only dates back to 1950 when FIDE released the first list of titled players.

Different times

Hard to believe in a time full of digital-era prodigies, but back then, on that first list, David Bronstein was the youngest GM at 26! His 'record' was broken by Tigran Petrosian at 23 in 1952, by Boris Spassky at 18 in 1955, and then, arguably the most impressive of all, by Bobby Fischer at the age of 15 in 1958.

Fischer's record stood the test of time for over 30 years before another sensational young teenager came on the scene. That he was a she as the all-time No 1 woman, Judit Polgar, hit the headlines by sensationally breaking the record in 1991. Over the next decade there followed a series of further holders of the youngest GM title – Peter Leko, Etienne Bacrot, Ruslan Ponomariov and Bu Xiangzhi – who all gradually lowered the age threshold before the next milestone moment, with Sergey Karjakin, in 2002, the first preteen to do so, aged just 12 years and 7 months.

The title became a launching pad for Karjakin's career, as he rose from prodigy to challenger for Magnus Carlsen's world crown in 2016. Interestingly, that title match was to be our first real introduction to a very young Abhi Mishra. Outside the New York venue for the match, father Hemant took what could prove to be a prophetic photograph on his smartphone, snapping his then 8-year-old son casually leaning against a Carlsen-Karjakin billboard.

An innocent enough snapshot that could well have been taken by any supportive father who was taking his son to his first major chess event, but now it sets us thinking if one day Abhi could well be gunning for Carlsen. And it cannot be denied that Karjakin has already fallen victim to him, as he smashed Sergey's long-standing record.

Sportingly, Karjakin had only kind words for the new record holder with his social media message: 'I am quite philosophical about this because it has been almost 20 years. It had to be broken sooner or later. I was sure one of the Indian guys would do it much earlier, and I was lucky that it didn't happen.

'I am a little sad that I lost the record, but at the same time I can only congratulate him and it's no problem. I hope that he will go on to be one of the top chess players and that it will be a nice start to his big career.'

Preparing for Magnus

By his own admission Abhi's biggest inspiration has been Magnus Carlsen. 'The way he's dominated the game since he's become World Champion, it's amazing.' And he further adds that he's not just grown up with Magnus, he's also grown up with his eponymous Play Magnus App! Of all the chess tools available now for kids to develop and hone their chess skills, that was the one he and his father singled out as being the most beneficial.

'I must have played over a thousand games with that app, always challenging and looking to better Magnus.' Indeed, as his father recalls it, he started when he was 5 and challenged himself by playing with month level options, such as 8 years and 1 month, 8 years and 2 months and so on, and kept moving up, the motivation being to always play and beat an older Carlsen than himself.

So what next for Abhi Mishra? While in Budapest, amidst all the media

A photo for the history books. Eight-year-old Abhi Mishra in New York during the Carlsen-Karjakin match.

hoopla, along came a wildcard entry to the FIDE World Cup in Sochi. There he'll meet the unpredictable and imaginative Baadur Jobava in the first round. And after the World Cup, it's the long homeward trek to New Jersey for a celebratory family reunion and to see his friends once again. He also admitted he needs a long rest after his exploits, 'at least two months away from chess,' confirms father Hemant.

And after a well-deserved rest, what then? Brimming with the exuberance of a young grandmaster who has just made history, he now wants to work with someone like Vladimir Kramnik to develop his game to the next level. He is determined to quickly establish himself as a 2700+ Super GM, confidently adding: 'I'm sure I can do this before I'm 15 – quite positive about this.' And with history-maker Abhi Mishra's track

record of setting himself challenges and beating age-record, just who would dare to bet against him?

Selected game

During his Budapest campaign Abhi Mishra played a stunning 70 games. From these he chose the following encounter as his best effort.

NOTES BY
Abhimanyu Mishra

Abhimanyu Mishra
Dey Shahil
Budapest Vezerkepzo 2021 (4)
Slav Defence

1.d4 d5 2.c4 c6 3.♘f3 ♘f6 4.♕b3 For this game, played in Round 4 of the Vezerkepzo GM Mix tournament in Budapest, I decided to surprise my opponent, so I went with 4.♕b3!?. **4...dxc4 5.♕xc4 ♗f5 6.g3 e6 7.♗g2 ♗e7 8.0-0 0-0** Up to here, it has been standard theory.

9.♘bd2!? The idea of ♘bd2 is to wait until Black commits himself to ...♘bd7 before White plays the ♕b3/♘c4 plan.
After the immediate 9.♕b3, 9...♕b6 10.♘bd2 ♖d8!? 11.♘c4 ♕a6 would be fine for Black, taking control of the d6-square.
9...♘bd7 10.♕b3 ♕b6 11.♘c4

Abhi not just grew up with Magnus, he also grew up with the Play Magnus App!

11...♕a6

The endgame after 11...♕xb3 12.axb3 is slightly better for White due to his pressure on the queenside and his knights controlling squares e5 and a5.

12.♗f4 ♘d5?!

Intending to take on e7 with the knight after White trades the dark-squared bishops. It is slightly inaccurate. Better was 12...♘b6 13.♗d6 ♖fe8 14.♗xe7 ♖xe7 15.♖fc1, when the position is close to equal.

13.♗d6 ♗e4

14.♗xe7!?

The engine prefers to leave the bishop on d6 and continue with a move like 14.♖fc1, but this forcing solution appealed to me during the game.

14...♘xe7 15.♘d6 ♗d5 16.♕c2

16...♘c8?! This is too passive. 16...♘f6! would have been only marginally better for White: 17.e4 ♖ad8 18.e5 ♘e8 19.♘g5 g6 20.♗xd5 cxd5 21.♘xe8 ♖dxe8 22.♕d2.

17.♘g5 Provoking a weakness on the black kingside.

17...♘f6

18.♘de4! Not trading the knight for the lousy knight on c8.

18...♘xe4 19.♗xe4 ♗xe4?!

Now White gets serious attacking chances. Better was 19...h6! 20.♗xd5 hxg5 21.♗f3, with only a bit of an edge for White.

20.♕xe4 g6 21.e3

Here 21.♕h4! h5 22.e4 ♕e2 23.♕f4 was even stronger than what I played.

21...h6 22.♘f3 Of course, 22.♘e6?? fails to 22...♖e8, and Black wins. And obviously not 22...fxe6?? 23.♕xg6+ ♔h8 24.♕xh6+ ♔g8 25.♕g6+ ♔h8 26.♖ac1, and Black can resign.

22...♕b5 23.♘e5 ♘e7 24.♕f4

24...♘f5? This fails to a very deep combination.

Black had to play 24...♔g7!, with the point of 25.♘d7 ♘d5 26.♕e5+ f6 27.♕xe6 ♖fe8 28.♕g4 b6!, when the knight is stranded on d7; but after

29.e4! ♖ad8 30.exd5 ♕xd5 31.♘xf6 White is still a pawn up.

25.a4! I didn't like 25.g4, in view of 25...g5 26.♕f3 ♘h4 27.♕f6 ♕d5 28.f3 ♔h7 29.♘xf7 ♘g6 30.e4 ♕b5, and now 31.♕xe6? fails to 31...♖ae8 32.♕f5 ♕b6, and Black is on top, because the white knight is lost.

25...♕a5 26.g4 g5 27.♕f3 ♘h4 28.♕f6 ♕d5 29.f3

29...♔h7 Somehow, after 29...c5!! White is only marginally better: 30.♕xh6 cxd4 31.♕xg5+ ♘g6 32.f4 dxe3 33.♖ae1 ♖ac8! 34.♖xe3 ♖c2 35.♖ef3 ♕e4! 36.♖1f2 ♕e1+ 37.♔g2 ♖xf2+ 38.♖xf2 ♕e4+ 39.♔g3

ANALYSIS DIAGRAM

39...♔g7!! (there is no time for

Smyslov, Bronstein, Geller, Taimanov and Averbakh. *A Chess Multibiography with 220 Games.* Andrew Soltis. NEWLY PUBLISHED. 2021, $65 library binding (18.4 × 26 cm), 392pp., 44 photographs, 227 diagrams, appendices, notes, bibliography, indexes, 978-1-4766-7793-4. Explores how fate played a capricious role in the lives of five of the greatest players in chess history.

Tal, Petrosian, Spassky and Korchnoi. *A Chess Multibiography with 207 Games.* Andrew Soltis. 2020 [original lib. bdg. 2019], $39.95 now softcover (17.8 × 25.4 cm), 394pp., 30 photographs, appendices, notes, bibliography, indexes, 978-1-4766-8364-5. The intense rivalry— and collaboration. "Arguably the best book Soltis has ever written"—IM John Donaldson. BOOK OF THE YEAR AWARD—*Chess Journalists of America.*

Neumann, Hirschfeld and Suhle. *19th Century Berlin Chess Biographies with 711 Games.* Hans Renette and Fabrizio Zavatarelli. 2020 [original lib. bdg. 2018], $49.95 (21.9 × 28.5 cm), 382pp., 66 photographs, appendices, notes, bibliography, indexes, 978-1-4766-7379-0. "Impressive variety of sources"—*American Chess Magazine*; "lively ... interesting and enjoyable"—*Mind's Eye Press*; "Outstanding historical research."—*British Chess News.*

José Raúl Capablanca. *A Chess Biography.* Miguel A. Sánchez. 2015, $55 library binding (18.4 × 26 cm), 563pp., 195 annotated games, 55 illustrations, appendices, notes, bibliography, indexes, 978-0-7864-7004-4. "Amazing"—*Huffington Post;* "the most ardent fan will learn something"—*Chess Life*; "luxurious, a true labor of love"—*Chess News*; "first rate ... highly recommended"—IM John Donaldson.

Kurt Richter. *A Chess Biography with 499 Games.* Alan McGowan. 2018, $75 library binding (21.9 × 28.5 cm), 380pp., 93 photographs, appendices, notes, bibliography, indexes, 978-1-4766-6906-9. The life (1900–1969) and games. "Treasure trove of games and a wonderful overview ... 5 shining stars!"—*New in Chess*; "A model of what a game collection and biography should be ... highly recommended"—IM John Donaldson.

Louis Paulsen. *A Chess Biography with 719 Games.* Hans Renette. 2019, $75 library binding (21.9 × 28.5 cm), 448pp., 108 photographs, appendices, notes, bibliography, indexes, 978-1-4766-7195-6. "Definitive ... outstanding ... highly recommended"—IM John Donaldson.

IT'S YOUR MOVE! 28" × 28" OIL ON LINEN,
LOUIS MUNROE 2018 (DWAYNESUENO@GMAIL.COM)

Chess Rivals of the 19th Century. *With 300 Annotated Games.* Tony Cullen. NEWLY PUBLISHED. 2021, $45 softcover (17.8 × 25.4 cm), 477pp., 54 photographs, diagrams, games, bibliography, indexes, 978-1-4766-8072-9. Provides a comprehensive overview, with more than a third of the 300 annotated games analyzed by past masters and checked by powerful engines. Fifty masters are each given their own chapter, with brief biographies, results and anecdotes and an endgame section for most chapters.

A World of Chess. *Its Development and Variations through Centuries and Civilizations.* Jean-Louis Cazaux and Rick Knowlton. 2017, $49.95 softcover (17.8 × 25.4 cm), 408pp., 71 illus., 297 diagrams, 9 maps, notes, bibliography, indexes, 978-0-7864-9427-9. The Persian and Arab game for 500 years; games going back 1500 years; chess variants ("960," board sizes, new pieces, 3-D etc.). "Definitive"—IM John Donaldson; "impressive"—*Chessbook Reviews*; "wonderful and unique"—*Mind's Eye Press.*

Steinitz in London. *A Chess Biography with 623 Games.* Tim Harding. $75 library binding (21.9 × 28.5 cm), 421pp., 84 photographs, appendices, notes, bibliography, indexes, 978-1-4766-6953-3. New research, early life and career, all known games until he left London in 1882.

Alexander Alekhine's Chess Games, 1902–1946. *2543 Games of the Former World Champion, Many Annotated by Alekhine, with 1868 Diagrams, Fully Indexed.* Leonard M. Skinner and Robert G.P. Verhoeven. 2019 [original lib. bdg. 1998], $59.95 now softcover in 2 vols. (21.9 × 28.5 cm), 824pp., 1,868 diagrams, references, bibliography, indexes, 978-1-4766-7942-6. HISTORICAL BOOK OF THE YEAR—U.S. Chess Federation. FINALIST, BOOK OF THE YEAR—British Chess Federation.

Mikhail Botvinnik. *The Life and Games of a World Chess Champion.* Andrew Soltis. 2014, $55 library binding (18.4 × 26 cm), 284pp., 128 diagrams, 12 photographs, chronology, appendices, notes, bibliography, indexes, 978-0-7864-7337-3. "Brilliant ... the best book on Botvinnik by far"—*Chess News.* BOOK OF THE YEAR—English Chess Federation. BOOK OF THE YEAR AWARD—*Chess Journalists of America.* FINALIST, BOOK OF THE YEAR—*Chess Cafe.*

Aron Nimzowitsch. *On the Road to Chess Mastery, 1886–1924.* Per Skjoldager and Jørn Erik Nielsen. 2012, $55 library binding (18.4 × 26 cm), 426 annotated games, 88 photographs, 10 maps, appendices, notes, bibliography, indexes, 978-0-7864-6539-2. "Magnificent...surpasses everything else we have ever seen"—*Chess.* BOOK OF THE YEAR—*Chess Cafe.*

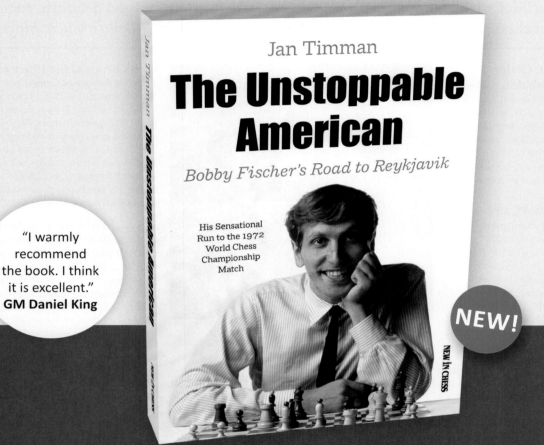

38.g5! A strong move based on the tactic that we will see in the game.

Typically, Abhi's day is filled with chess and chess, but there was a little bit of time for sightseeing in Hungary as well.

39...♕e3+? 40.♘f3 ♚g7 41.f5!, and White is winning) 40.h4 ♕e3+ 41.♘f3, and now Black has 41...f6!, and holds. But of course this is very difficult, if not impossible, to calculate and evaluate correctly over the board.

30.♘xf7 ♚g6 31.e4

31...♕b3

31...♕a5? loses to 32.f4! gxf4 33.♖a3!! (the point of 25.a4) 33...♕c7 34.♘g5+ hxg5 35.♖h3+ ♘h4 36.♕xg5, and Black will be mated.

32.f4!! With this pawn push, White clears the third rank for the rook. 32.♖a3? is premature and won't work, in view of 32...♕xb2 and the road to h3 is blocked.

32...♕e3+

Taking the pawn 32...gxf4? now loses to 33.♖a3! ♕xb2 34.♖h3.

33.♖f2 gxf4 34.♖a3 ♕e1+ 35.♖f1

35...♕h4

35...♕e2 was another option, hoping for 36.♘g5+? (36.♖af3!, followed by pushing the h-pawn, wins) 36...hxg5 37.♖h3+ ♘h4 38.♕xg5?? (38.♖xh4+! gxh4 39.♕xh4+ would still be a draw) 38...♕g2, mate.

36.♕xh4 ♘xh4 37.♖xf4! ♚g7

38...hxg5? This just loses. The computer suggests 38...h5!! 39.♖xh4 ♖xf7 40.♖xh5 ♖f4!, with compensation for Black due to the bad position of the white rooks. **39.♘xg5! ♖xf4 40.♘xe6+ ♚f6 41.♘xf4**

White is two pawns up without any compensation on Black's part. The rest is easy conversion.

41...♘g5 42.♘e2 ♖e8 43.♖g3+ ♚f6 44.♖g4 ♘f3+ 45.♚f2 ♘d2 46.e5+ ♚e6 47.♚e3 ♘c4+ 48.♚e4 ♘d2+ 49.♚d3 ♘f3 50.♖g7 c5 51.♘f4+ ♚f5 52.♖f7+ ♚g4 53.♘d5

Black resigned. ∎

Mamedyarov's Hattrick

Azeri GM wins Superbet Classic in Bucharest

A flash in the pan of three subsequent wins sufficed for Shakhriyar Mamedyarov to claim the Superbet Classic and take home the $90,000 winner's fee. The eagerly awaited first leg of the 2021 Grand Chess Tour got off to a cautious start and invoked criticism with a disturbing number of lame draws. GCT commentator **CRISTIAN CHIRILA** was happy to return to Bucharest and shares his enthusiasm about the beginning of a warm chess summer.

Last year, the Grand Chess Tour was one of many prominent chess events to fall victim to the pandemic. Fortunately, when the world was slowly opening up again at the beginning of this year, rumours started circulating about a potential return of the Tour, and in spite of countless logistical challenges, that is exactly what happened.

The first leg of the 2021 Tour was scheduled to take place in Bucharest, Romania, in June. There were lots of concerned voices, but in the end the organizers were able to overcome all hurdles (and there were many) and put on a chess spectacle craved by fans around the world.

The Grand Chess Tour is a series of invitational elite grandmaster events. Two of them, the Superbet Classic in Bucharest and the Sinquefield Cup in St. Louis in August, are classical tournaments. The three other legs, in Paris, Croatia and St. Louis (preceding the Sinquefield Cup), are Rapid & Blitz tournaments.

I have been working for the Grand Chess Tour for a few years now, and when I was invited to join the commentary team for the Superbet Chess Classic, I accepted without any hesitation. I was going to visit my home country and commentate on the games of the best chess players on the planet. Was there a better way to start the summer?

Last-minute changes
Little more than a week before the start of the event, a series of critical roster changes had to be made when it became clear that Ding Liren and Viswanathan Anand could not make it to Bucharest. Due to visa issues, the Chinese number 3 in the world was forced to withdraw from the Tour. Quickly there was confirmation about his replacement as a full Tour participant by Richard Rapport, the talented and uncompromising 25-year-old Hungarian grandmaster. While Richard has not been very active in the past few years, he still managed to reach his peak rating of 2763 in February of this year. Due to the worsening Covid-19 situation in India, Anand was unable to travel to Romania. Constantin Lupulescu, the number one Romanian player, was given the opportunity to compete against the best in the world, giving the local fans a personal hero to root for!

Then, only two days before the start of the event, another piece fell off the organizers' chessboard when Rapport suddenly had to withdraw from the competition due to illness. Looking for a last-minute replacement, the organizers quickly turned their attention to the young Romanian prodigy Bogdan Deac. The 18-year-old (who turned 19 during the tournament) is Romania's generational talent. He became a Grandmaster at only 14 years of age and has since been steadily climbing the world rankings. This was Bogdan's first opportunity to prove his mettle against the best players in the world, and proving it was exactly what he did!

Palpable excitement
The Superbet Classic started on a sunny Saturday afternoon, and the excitement in the playing hall was palpable. The local media and fans were present, trying to catch every move and gesture of the main protagonists. The stage was set for the players to arrive and start what was symbolically the beginning of a new chapter in competitive over-the-board chess after a difficult hiatus that lasted more than a year.

While most of the games were not particularly tense, one could feel the excitement and overall eagerness of the players to once again be facing and sensing each other's presence across the board. Despite the general peaceful tone of the round, there was one game that captured the public's attention, the clash between Bogdan Deac and Anish Giri, an intriguing game, particularly because neither

Bogdan Deac, Romania's biggest promise, who turned 19 during the tournament, proved his mettle in his debut in an elite event.

player pulled any punches when given the opportunity. Giri decided to steer the game into a sharp Semi-Slav, and Deac welcomed the dangerous complications with open arms. After a tense middlegame, Deac was able to garner a sizable advantage, and even had a golden opportunity to take Giri down.

Bogdan-Daniel Deac
Anish Giri
Bucharest 2021 (1)

position after 28...c5

29.♕d7+?! A normal-looking decision, but there was something much better: 29.♖e5! is a typical rook swing to bring the last attacker into the game, but the real point of this shot is only revealed on the next move. 29...♕xg3 (the most critical response, which from afar looks as if it will allow Black to find enough counterplay) 30.♖h5!! (30.♖xc5?! must be what the players had calculated, and made White decide that it does not offer enough winning chances: 30...♕xd6 31.♖xd6 ♗xf3 32.gxf3 ♖d8, and Black has good chances to hold).

ANALYSIS DIAGRAM

Once you see this blow, it becomes obvious that Black no longer has a defence: 30...♕xd6 31.♖xh8+ ♔d7 32.♖xd6+ ♔xd6 33.♗xb7, and White is a rook up and should be able to convert with ease.

Garry Kasparov was on the official live broadcast and did not want to leave the analysis before Deac would have made the critical 29th move. After the Romanian youngster had missed this golden opportunity, Giri defended well.

29...♔b8 30.♗xb7 ♔xb7 31.♖xe6 ♕xg3

Now Black gets enough counterplay to force the queen trade and force a transition to a balanced endgame.

Garry Kasparov, a frequent visitor to the live broadcast, followed the games with his usual passion.

LENNART OOTES

32.♕c6+ ♔b8 33.♕d6 ♕xd6 34.♖exd6 ♔b7 35.♖f6 ♖h7 36.♖d7 b4 37.axb4 cxb4 38.♔f2 a5 Black's queenside pawns provide the counterplay he needs.
39.♔e2 ♖g7 40.♖fxf7 ♖xg2+ 41.♔d1 ♖g1+ 42.♔c2 ♖g2+

White cannot walk out of the rook checks, since the king would be mated on a4 by ...♖a3 mate, so a repetition becomes inevitable.
43.♔b1 ♖g1+ 44.♔b2 ♖g2+ 45.♔b1 ♖g1+ 46.♔b2 ♖g2+ 47.♔b1 ♖g1+ Draw.

A key moment for the Romanian talent came in Round 2, when he faced Maxime Vachier-Lagrave with the black pieces. While the opening did not go particularly well, Bogdan

defended tenaciously and managed to hold off his formidable opponent when the decisive moment was reached.

**Maxime Vachier-Lagrave
Bogdan-Daniel Deac**
Bucharest 2021 (2)

position after 29...g6

White is better due to his more active pieces, and the better safety of his king. It was at this moment that MVL's tournament went astray after the horrendous:
30.♕d3?
A completely inexplicable lapse of judgement from one of the best players in the world.

Instead, 30.♕e6!, forcing Black to continue defending, was the way to go. Black now needs to bring his queen back in order to protect against White's kingside offensive, starting with the threat of ♕xg6. 30...♕g7 31.♘g3 ♖ad8 32.♗c2 ♘e7 33.♘h5!

ANALYSIS DIAGRAM

with a devastating attack.
30...♖f5!
Now Black takes over the initiative, as there is no way to defend against the

capture of the important g5-pawn, which dominated the black knight and allowed White to launch his offensive.

31.♕c3+ ♕xc3 32.♖xc3 ♖xg5+ 33.♘g3 ♘f6 34.♔f1 ♖b8 35.h3 ♖e5 36.♗c4 ♖c5 37.♖cc2 ♖a5

Black has easy play, and White has no targets. The rest is easy.
38.♘e4 ♘xe4 39.♖xe4 ♖xa4 40.h4 ♔g7 41.h5 gxh5 42.♖e1 ♖bb4 43.♗e2 ♖h4 44.♗f3 a5
White resigned.

These are the types of wins that allow a young player to grow tenfold in confidence. Only time will tell whether this was Bogdan's break-through moment.

Another crucial moment came in Round 4, when the two Americans, Wesley So and Fabiano Caruana, met in a mouthwatering clash. Wesley had had a quiet event up to that point, drawing all his games without much labour. Fabiano was co-leading after making good use of his white pieces against Lupulescu in Round 2. Both players came out swinging.

NOTES BY
Anish Giri

**Wesley So
Fabiano Caruana**
Bucharest 2021 (4)
English Opening, Reversed Sicilian

1.c4 Wesley So afterwards explained his choice of opening, saying that it was a little easier to predict what would happen here, as opposed to 1.d4 or 1.e4, after each of which, he said, Fabiano plays five different openings. Solid reasoning!
1...e5 2.g3 ♘f6 3.♗g2

3...♗c5 Fabi used to play the 3...c6 system a lot, but decided to mix things up a little bit for this game. This system has also been trendy for a couple of years.
4.d3 A topical move. After 4.♘c3 c6 5.♘f3 e4 things get very messy, whereas this continuation usually postpones the crisis.
4...c6 This is also how Vishy Anand played against me in the Kolkata Rapid 2019. It was a very memorable game, as I got completely outplayed by the Indian legend until, shockingly, he lost on time.
5.♘f3 d6 6.0-0 0-0 7.♘c3 a5
This is also how Vishy played against me. Wang Hao chose 7...♖e8 against Ding in the Candidates in 2020.

8.d4!? I played the slow 8.b3 against

The mouth-watering clash between the two Americans in the field, Wesley So and Fabiano Caruana, ended in a fine victory for the first player.

Erling Tholfsen: 'Do whatever you can to discourage him, Mrs. Fischer.' *(The advice given in a letter sent by the US Chess Official to a mother who said her young boy was interested in chess, and what should she do?)*

Andrew Soltis: 'During an international tournament, time often passes at the rate of dog years - one week with grandmasters can seem like seven weeks with other people.' *(Observed in his witty autobiography, Confessions of a Chess Grandmaster)*

Agatha Christie: 'I don't think even a Russian would murder another man in order not to be beaten at chess.' *(From one of her crime novels featuring Hercule Poirot, The Big Four)*

Karen Carney: 'It's like a chess match - neither side is making the first move.' *(A puzzling remark from the BT Sport broadcaster, said during May's English Premier League match-up between Manchester Utd and Liverpool)*

Julian Barnes: 'Chess is a luck-free zone.' *(From his book, Letters from London 1990-1995)*

Randall Jarrell: 'Compare the saint who, asked what he would do if he had only an hour to live, replied that he would go on with his game of chess, since it was as much worship as anything else he had ever done.' *(The American poet, essayist and novelist in his 1979 book, Kipling, Auden and Co.: Essays and Reviews, 1935-1964)*

Ulf Andersson: 'All my losses are bitter. (..) I suppose all players suffer when they lose. When you put your heart in something and when it does not go how you wish, then you suffer.' *(The legendary Swedish Grandmaster, who recently celebrated his 70th birthday)*

Bill Dunphy: '[Ulf] Andersson's style consists in playing chess backwards!' *(The Hastings congress tournament director in the mid-1970s, on the playing style of the Swede)*

Albert 'Boxbox' Zheng: 'He blew my mind with how deep chess goes.' *(The American full-time 'League of Legends' superstar streamer, interviewed in Wire magazine about the growth of chess on Twitch during the lockdown, and being inspired to play more after meeting Hikaru Nakamura)*

Robert Pirsig: 'Chess is the triumph of mental organisation over complex experience.' *(The American writer famous for his novel Zen and the Art of Motorcycle Maintenance)*

Alexander Khalifman: 'Necessary disclaimer: I believe that these questions were sent to me mistakenly. I'm no legend at all, just an average level player. Some reputable experts insist even that my level was far below average. Maybe they're right, but I'm not so sure.' *(The Russian's self-effacing introduction to the 'Legends Questions' in the ECU's Newsletter)*

Prof. Robert Desjarlais: 'Chess reflects how people long for meaning and purpose in their lives, how we want to live intensely, craft something of beauty, test ourselves against others, and achieve a sense of mastery in our own endeavours.' *(In the chess-loving academic's 2012 book, Counterplay: An Anthropologist at the Chessboard)*

Tim Krabbé: 'Anyone can hang a piece, but a good blunder requires thought.' *(The chess-playing Dutch author, famous for his novel The Vanishing)*

Deirdre Lawson: 'I feel like I'm playing chess, human chess. And it's always a moving chessboard.' *(The Atlanta conflict analyst, interviewed on CNN on Covid reopening anxieties and logistics in the US)*

Anish Giri: 'In this day and age, with people knowing so much theory, the definition of 'risk' is changing to some extent. There are no more risky lines that nobody has studied. The Trompowsky everybody knows, 1.b3 people also know, and if you play the King's Gambit… well, it's an insane risk.'

Anand, and didn't get much going out of the opening. Wesley goes for the engine recommendation and opens up the centre.

8...exd4 9.♘xd4

An interesting position. White can claim some space in the centre, but Black is not without counterplay.

9...a4!?

An important strategic achievement, not letting White cement his c4-pawn with b3, exploiting the fact that ♘xa4 is impossible now due to ...♗xd4 and ...♖xa4. Now, if White is to ever play b3, which he will probably like to in order to support the c4-pawn, Black will open the a-file with ...axb3, activating his a8-rook, or trading it. In a cramped position, which is what Black has right now, any trades should be to his advantage.

10.♖b1 10.e3 a3 bothered Wesley, which is why he started with ♖b1, wanting to meet ...a3 with b4.

10...♖e8 The rook clearly belongs on the semi-open e-file.

11.e3 Guarding the d4-knight one more time and hinting at ♘xa4.

11...♕a5 The only way to protect the a4-pawn, although I have to say

it is hard to like this move, since the queen feels rather out of place here. 11...♗g4!? was more clever, setting up a pawn sacrifice: 12.f3 ♗c8!?. Black can simply drop the bishop back. 12...♗e6, which was mentioned by Wesley and leads to some simplifications, was very possible as well. 13.♘xa4, and now Black starts dynamic action: 13...♗xd4 14.exd4 ♗e6 15.b3 b5! (fighting for some light squares) 16.cxb5 cxb5 17.♘c3 b4, and Black is going to enjoy the d5-square, while White's pieces are rather poorly positioned here. Black has full compensation for his one pawn, the absence of which is barely felt.

12.♗d2 ♗g4 13.f3

13...♗h5?! Too risky. Later on, Black will regret having this bishop cut out of play. It was perfectly sensible to drop the bishop back to c8 now, having provoked the ugly f3 move, closing the view for the g2-bishop. 13...♗c8!? looks too provocative, but in fact, the bishop is better off on this diagonal, and spending two tempi to provoke that f3 weakening is quite worth it.

14.♘e4!

Drawing conclusions

While Shakhriyar Mamedyarov's three wins inevitably got the fans talking about how exciting chess can be, the Superbet Classic also rekindled the discussion about tacitly agreed insipid draws. Recently, this phenomenon was mainly associated with online rapid chess. Now we were watching an in-person classical tournament, and here, too, many games ended in draws with very little or no fighting. It wasn't the cold fact that only 27 per cent of the games were decided that troubled the fans, but the way many of these draws came about.

The main 'offender' was Teimour Radjabov, who started with a draw against Caruana,

Teimour Radjabov

playing moves that everyone had seen before and then also drew the rest of his games, leaving the impression that in most of them the predictable result was fine with him. As is known, such disregard of the spectators often rubs off. Typically, the draw that Mamedyarov went for in the penultimate round against Giri's Grünfeld, was identical to the draw Radjabov had played against MVL in Round 2. Radjabov had little understanding for the criticism he was subjected to, citing a crazy schedule with too many games. And tweeting: 'You may not like me. I don't care, honestly, but every chess player and someone that loves the game, is friend to me. Don't forget it! I am part of chess history, like it or not!'

The discussion about 'empty' draws is an important one in a sport that heavily depends on sponsorship. Teimour Radjabov first entered chess history many years ago in Linares, where legendary organizer Luis Rentero used to say: 'Players prepared to settle for a quick draw are welcome to do so at home, for their own money.' (DJtG)

14...♕d8 The engines also propose allowing the doubling of the f-pawns with 14....♕b6!?, but for most players this would be too ugly a solution.
15.♘xc5 dxc5 16.♘e2 ♕d3

White has some long-term advantages, e.g. the bishop pair, the better pawn structure and above all the h5-bishop going to be out of play. In return, Fabiano must have been pinning his hopes on this move, hitting the c4-pawn and having some ...♘e4!? ideas as well.

17.♘f4!
A powerful reply. It turns out that the c4-pawn is not all that crucial, and White gets a beautiful position in return.
17...♕xc4 18.b3

Sending the queen to a rather awkward square.
18...axb3 19.axb3 ♕b5
The queen is far away from the action, with the c6/c5-pawns serving as a wall.
20.e4 ♗g6 21.♗c3

21...♘a6?
This is just too much. Black divides the board into two halves, with the queen and the knight on the left, but on the right he is dead lost, especially with the powerful c3-bishop staring down the diagonal and the g6-bishop out of play. The idea is to get some counterplay with ...♘b4, but Black will be too late, as Wesley now starts playing super-accurately.
21...♘bd7! had to be tried, for better or worse, although White is still fully in control after 22.♕d2 ♕b6 23.♗b2 with, strategically speaking, a very bad position for Black. Black also has no real way to relieve the pressure, no breakthroughs or trades and at this point things have gone quite obviously wrong already.
22.h4!

Asking the right question: how is Black going to deal with the threat of ♗xf6 and h5?
22...h5 Necessary, but it does soften up Black's poor kingside even further.
23.♕c1! When I saw this move flashed out by Wesley, I instantly knew this was the one. Too elegant; and there also is the threat of ♕h6 after trading on g6 and f6.

WHY PLAY WHEN YOU DON'T NEED TO?

NOT ONLY DO WE TEACH YOU SEVERAL FORCED DRAWS IN THE BERLIN...

..BUT ALSO EARLY REPETITIONS IN THE ITALIAN, GRÜNFELD AND MANY OTHERS!

LAZY LIFETIME REPERTOIRE

BEREND VONK

23...♔h7

24.♖d1!
Another powerful move. Rushing in with 24.♕b2? would be a huge mistake, since this would allow 24...♘b4!, with the idea of ...♖a2, which is what Fabi must have been counting on.
24...♖ad8 Black didn't have any defence at this point, but this allows ♕b2, pretty much deciding the game in White's favour.
25.♕b2! c4
Black is trying to muddy the waters, but to no avail.
26.♗xf6 gxf6 27.♕xf6 ♖xd1+ 28.♖xd1

White has a crushing attack and Black has no time to proceed with his queenside counterplay.
28...♕c5+ 29.♔h2 ♕e7
Fabiano switches to defence, but now White is going to be up a pawn in the endgame, and even more importantly, he has four vs two on the kingside, meaning there are no drawing tendencies at all, since White will be able to create two passed pawns there in the long run.
30.♕xe7 ♖xe7 31.bxc4

White has a completely winning endgame. Wesley converts smoothly.
31...♔g7 32.♗h3 ♘c5 33.♖d6 f6 34.♘e6+ Trading knights is very clean. **34...♘xe6 35.♗xe6 ♗e8 36.c5**

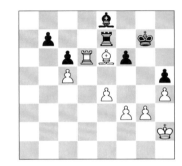

Black's queenside majority is completely neutralized, while White has 4 vs 2 on the other side of the board and will easily win any endgame.
36...♗f7 37.♗c8
The rook ending is obviously also winning, but Wesley goes for more. The b7-pawn is now doomed as well.
37...♖e5 Heading towards four vs two for lack of a better move.
38.♗xb7 ♖xc5 39.♖xc6

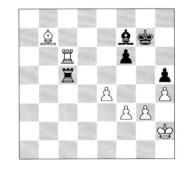

For a player of Wesley's calibre the rest is just autopilot.

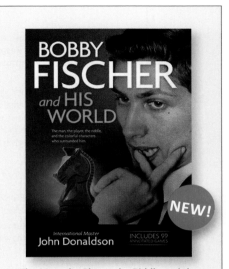

NEW IN CHESS bestsellers

Start Playing an Unsidesteppable & Low Maintenance Response to 1.e4 and Simultaneously Improve Your Chess Technique
Thomas Willemze

"This is a real gem! It's almost as if each annotation specifies the key strategic elements that uphold the assessments and choice of plans. A repertoire apt for club players, offering lessons in strategy, plus antidotes to seemingly troublesome White tries."
GM Glenn Flear

Creating a Plan that Works... and Sticking to It!
Davorin Kuljasevic

Stop wasting time and energy! Kuljasevic explains how to optimize your learning process, how to develop good study habits and get rid of useless ones, and what study resources are appropriate for players of different levels.

"I recommend this book unconditionally, it will be the standard work on studying chess for years."
Barry Braeken, Schaaksite

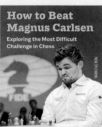

A Manual for Modern-Day Club Players
Gerard Welling & Steve Giddins

Will dramatically boost your skills – without carrying the excess baggage that many of your opponents will be struggling with.

"Aimed at amateur players who don't have much time to study."
IM Gary Lane, Chess Moves Magazine

"A refreshing attempt at producing s chess manual with a difference." – *Sean Marsh, CHESS Magazine*

Fresh Strategies and Resources for Dynamic Chess Players   *Viktor Moskalenko*

Viktor Moskalenko presents countless improvements, alternatives, new ideas and fresh weapons that will delight and surprise the reader, in his beloved French. As always, his analysis is high-level, yet his touch is light and fresh. Lots of original and dynamic options in every main line. A typical Moskalenko book: practical, accessible, original, entertaining and inspiring.

Exploring the Most Difficult Challenge in Chess
Cyrus Lakdawala

This fascinating book has a thematic structure, which, together with Lakdawala's uniquely accessible style, makes its lessons easy to digest. Sometimes even Magnus gets outplayed, sometimes he over-presses and goes over the cliff's edge, and sometimes he fails to find the correct plan. Lakdawala explains the how and the why.

A Practical Guide to a Vital Skill in Chess
Merijn van Delft

"Excellent examples. Will have a major impact on your positional progress."
IM Gary Lane, Chess Moves Magazine

"A grandmaster-level skill explained in a comprehensible and readable fashion."
GM Matthew Sadler

"Masterfully discusses a vital topic, to bring your chess to the next level." – *GM Karsten Müller*

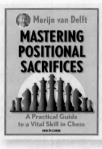

Improve Your Ability to Spot Typical Mates
Vladimir Barsky

"A fun way to instantly improve."
IM Gary Lane, ECF Newsletter

"The author knows exactly what he's doing and why he's doing it: something that can't be said for the majority of instructional chess books. If you're rated anywhere between about 1250 and 2000 and want to improve your attacking skills you'll find this book invaluable."
Richard James, British Chess News

AlphaZero's Groundbreaking Chess Strategies and the Promise of AI
Matthew Sadler & Natasha Regan

2019 Averbakh-Boleslavsky Award
ECF 2019 Book of the Year

"Quite inspirational." – *Magnus Carlsen*

"Once you experience the power of these ideas in your own game, you realise how much we can learn from the playing style of AlphaZero."
IM Stefan Kuipers

"This is a phenomenal book." – *IM John Bartholomew*

How to Save Points from Lost Positions
David Smerdon   ECF 2020 Book of the Year

"Combines insightful discussion of a previously unexplored subject, with good writing and great entertainment throughout." – *ECF Judges*

"Terrific examples and explanations. I have to recommend it to every chess friend, because the next lost position may come sooner than expected!" – *IM Dirk Schuh*

"A thrilling guide." – *GM Luke McShane, Spectator*

Vital Lessons for Every Chess Player
Jesus de la Villa

"If you've never read an endgame book before, this is the one you should start with."
GM Matthew Sadler, former British Champion

"If you really have no patience for endgames, at least read *100 Endgames You Must Know*."
Gary Walters Chess

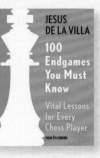

available at your local (chess)bookseller or at www.newinchess.com

39...罩b5 40.皇a6 罩b2+ 41.當g1
The king is briefly cut off along the second rank, but will inevitably move up slowly.
41...皇e8 42.罩c5 當h6 43.當f1 皇d7 44.皇e2

Clearing the second rank for the king.
44...皇e8 45.當f2 罩b3 46.罩d5 罩a3 47.皇d3 Also clearing the third rank for the king. **47...當g7 48.當e3 罩b3 49.當f4 罩b4 50.罩c5 皇f7 51.罩c7 當g6 52.g4**

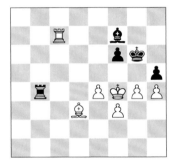

The final breakthrough, forcing resignation. Black resigned.

■ ■ ■

Mamedyarov takes over
And then Round 5 came, and together with it arrived hurricane Mamedyarov. The Azeri grandmaster had drawn his first four games and had told me in an interview that he was just 'warming up' after the long pause. The unprecedented break had ignited a fire that could be seen in his eyes. What he was looking for most was to get back to the board and enjoy the process – the result was only an afterthought. This is the

Shakhriyar was going to bring the fight to his opponents, and the next three rounds showed what that meant

type of mood that makes a player dangerous. Shakhriyar was going to bring the fight to his opponents, and the next three rounds showed what that meant.

The first game he won was against Lupulescu, the Romanian wildcard who had just beaten Giri in Round 3. Mamedyarov opted for a peculiar opening set-up, slowly but surely managing to push his opponent into muddy waters, where he managed to finally take over.

Constantin Lupulescu
Shakhriyar Mamedyarov
Bucharest 2021 (5)

position after 31...罩g8

The situation is extremely tense. Black's pieces have more flexibility, and despite the assessment 'equal' by the computer, this position is much easier to play as Black from a human perspective. At this point, Lupulescu was also in some difficulty on the clock, having only a few minutes left to reach the time-control.
32.皇e2?!
Going into the wrong direction.
A better way to fight Black's initiative was 32.奂e5!?:

A) After 32...奂h5?

ANALYSIS DIAGRAM

the point of having the knight on e5 becomes clear, as the attack on g3 will easily be parried due to the vulnerability of the f7-pawn: 33.皇e2 豐xg3+?? (and 33...奂xg3?? 34.罩g1 simply wins a piece for White) 34.豐xg3 奂xg3 35.奂xf7+ loses for Black.

B) 32...奂d5 33.奂c4 罩dd8 34.皇g2, and without the rook on d6 ready to swing over to the sixth rank, Black will have a very difficult task developing his attack.
32...奂d5

33.皇f1?
After another weak move, the position is almost hopeless for White, at least practically speaking. Shakhriyar Mamedyarov now goes on to display his fearsome attacking instincts.
White was already running out of time, but reinforcing the critical g3-square with 33.罩g1! was crucial, when after 33...e5 34.fxe5 奂xe5 35.奂h4 奂e7 36.罩bd1 the situation is not clear yet.
33...e5! 34.fxe5??

Allowing Black to do what he wanted to do.

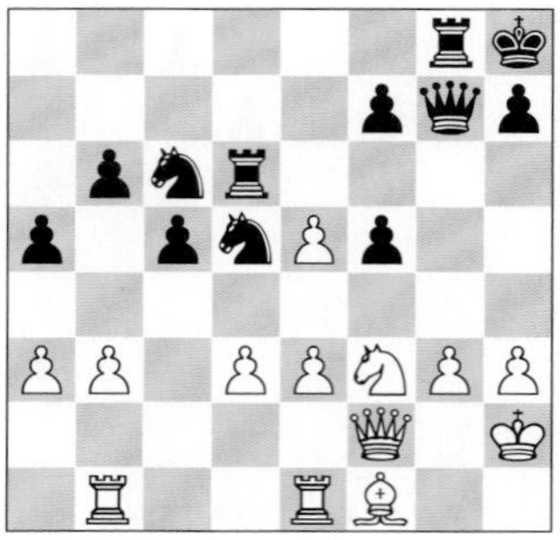

34...♖g6! Now it's all over, as Black's pieces will pierce through White's feeble defence.
35.♘h4 ♖xg3 36.d4 After 36.♘xf5 Black has 36...♖f3!!,

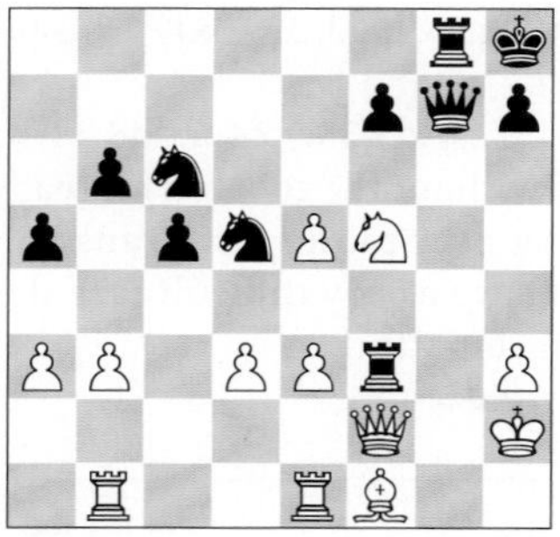

a beautiful idea that Lupulescu had missed from afar: 37.♕xf3 ♕g1 mate.
36...♕g5 37.♘g2 cxd4 38.exd4 ♘xd4

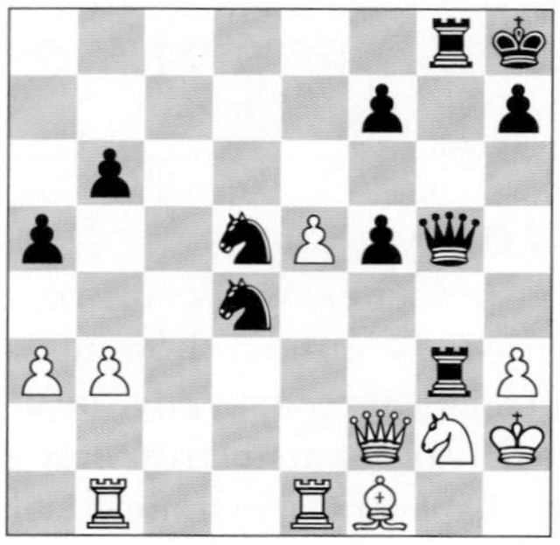

White resigned. A critical victory that jumpstarted Mamedyarov's quest for the title.

After beating Levon Aronian in Round 6, Mamedyarov faced another difficult test against Fabiano Caruana, with the black pieces. With a fine win Shakhriyar managed to distance himself from the pack and take a commanding lead into the final two rounds.

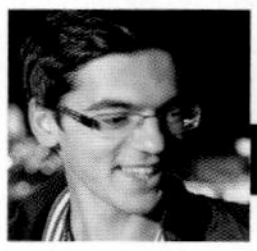

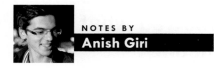

NOTES BY
Anish Giri

Fabiano Caruana
Shakhriyar Mamedyarov
Bucharest 2021 (7)
Ruy Lopez, Berlin Defence

1.e4 e5 2.♘f3 ♘c6 3.♗b5 ♘f6

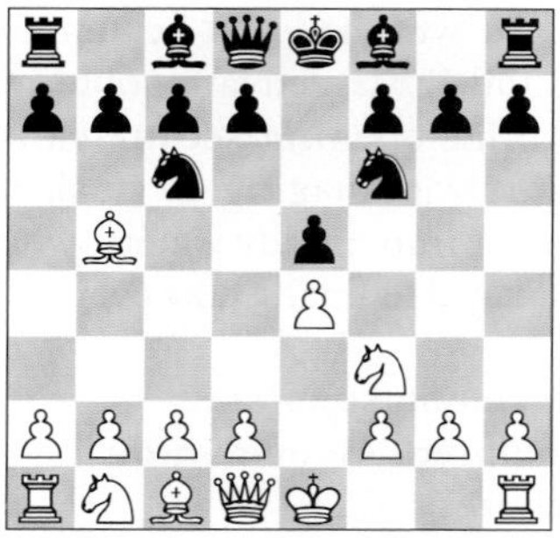

The Berlin is a very rare guest in the practice of Shakhriyar Mamedyarov. I thought he had never played it before, but upon checking the database, I was reminded that he did; a few years back against Karjakin and Hou Yifan in the World Cup. Still, Fabiano was certainly taken aback by this.

I don't think there is a variation against the Berlin that Fabiano hasn't tried

4.d3 Against me, Fabiano Caruana tried 4.0-0 ♘xe4 5.d4 ♘d6 6.♗xc6 dxc6 7.dxe5 ♘f5 8.♕e2!?, but against a well-prepared opponent, it is no wonder that Fabiano decided not to repeat this and try something else.

4...♗c5 5.♘c3 A relatively rare move that Fabiano had played a few times before. At this point, I don't think there is a variation against the Berlin that Fabiano hasn't tried.
5...♘d4 Shakhriyar responds quickly and energetically.

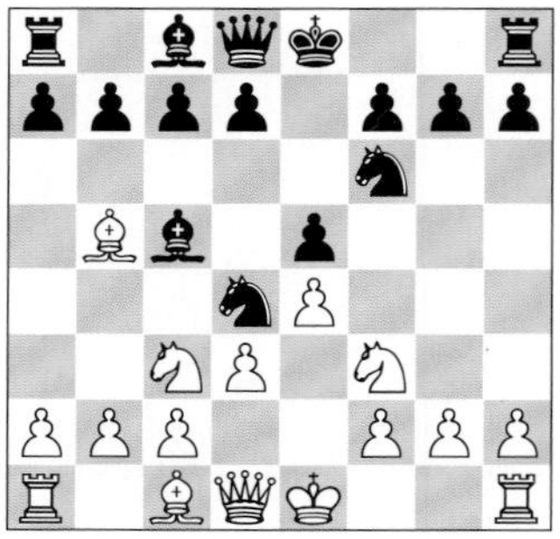

6.♗a4 White has a few options here, but this is not the most critical one. Fabiano probably wanted to get Shakh out of book, not wanting to test him in the complications after 6.♘xe5.
6...c6 7.0-0 d6 The question in these positions is often which player will trade knights first.
8.♘xd4 ♗xd4 9.h3 This is waving a red flag in front of a bull and could actually have been a brilliant trap...

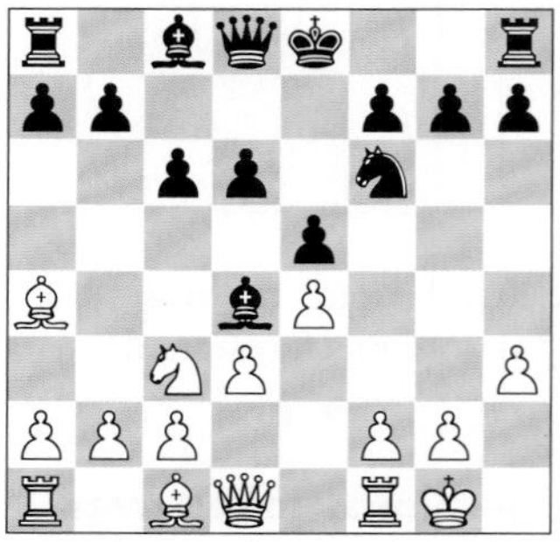

9...g5?!
Shakh goes for it. It is a common theme that when White has castled and gone for the creation of luft with h3, Black can often punish this with the hyper-aggressive ...g5 push. The most recent famous example that comes to mind is Aronian-Kramnik from the Berlin Candidates 2018, where I was seconding Kramnik and was thrilled to see him cruise against

such a formidable opponent in such spectacular style. I loved this push here as well, but when checking the game with the computer afterwards, I was surprised to notice a major flaw.

10.♘e2?

Surprisingly, Fabiano misses it as well. Now the ...g5 push is justified. Instead, there was 10.♘d5!.

ANALYSIS DIAGRAM

I don't recall seeing such a resource, but it works perfectly here. The threat is ♗xg5, but also c3, getting rid of the important dark-squared bishop. Now 10...♖g8 is objectively best, probably, but after this move White gets rid of the powerful bishop (10...♗d7 was Shakh's original intention, but this fails to work. 11.♗xg5! cxd5, and now the immediate 12.♕f3!, or 12.♗xd7+ first, wins back the piece with dividend, and it is White who remains on top in the end) 11.c3 ♗b6 12.♘xb6 axb6 13.♗e3, and White doesn't have much to fear. Without the bishop on the a7-g1 diagonal, the ...g4 push alone lacks punch, because ...g3 doesn't have the same force after h4, due to the lack of pressure on the f2-pawn.

10...♗b6

Shakhriyar Mamedyarov's most inspired effort from the hattrick that brought him tournament victory, was his black win against Fabiano Caruana.

11.c3?!

This feels too slow. Fabiano probably just didn't see anything better and decided to start defending.
11.♘g3!? looks more natural. After 11...g4 (11...♖g8 is more solid, but then White has good chances to weather the storm with 12.♗e3) Fabiano may have underestimated 12.♗g5, being only worried about 12.h4?, which runs into 12...♘h5!!. Now it's a mess.

11...♖g8 12.d4

White is hoping for some trades and some kind of safety.

12...♘xe4 13.♗c2 d5

14.♗xe4?!

Understandable temptation: cut your losses and try to defend the endgame. But the endgame is too unpleasant, and it was probably more promising to fish for chances in the muddy waters after 14.dxe5!?.

14...dxe4 15.dxe5 ♕xd1 16.♖xd1 g4!

In the endgame, too, the g-file is an issue for White.

17.h4 g3 18.♘d4

Fabiano must have missed or underestimated Shakh's next move.
18.♗e3!? would have offered better saving chances, as the move in the game runs into a mighty reply.

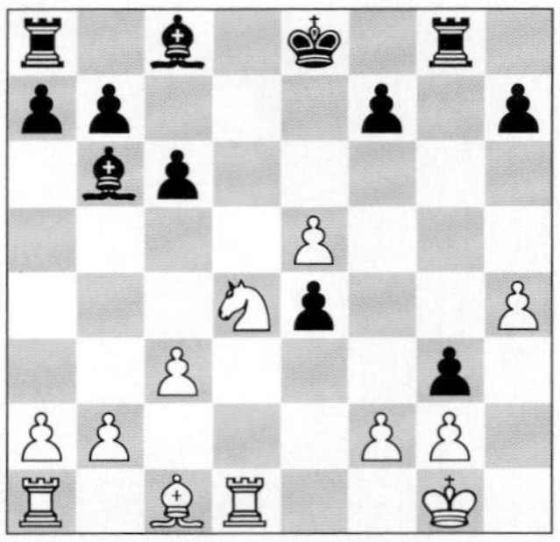

18...♗d8!

Brilliant. As soon as I saw it, it was clear to me that Fabiano was in serious trouble. It is key to prevent ♗g5 and stabilize the dark squares on the kingside. Now White can only do this at the cost of a pawn, if not two.

19.fxg3 ♖xg3

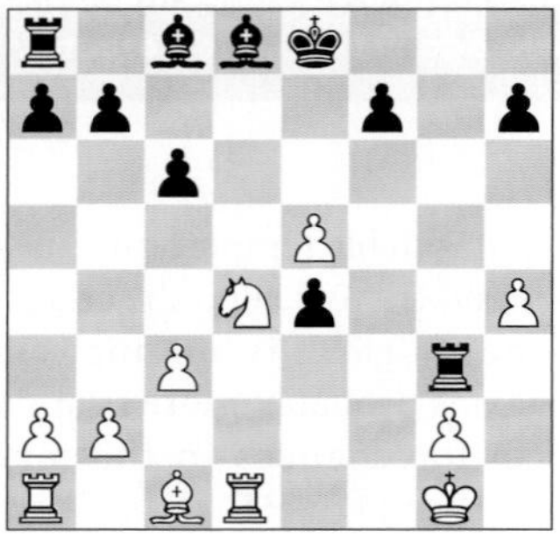

20.♖e1?

After a long think Fabiano comes up with what looks like a very good attempt at trying to settle for a somewhat worse but defendable position, but as Shakh continues with perfect moves, this just leads to a lost position.

It is hard to suggest anything, since White is clearly worse everywhere. But he should still have played something else.

20...♖g4! 21.♗g5 ♗xg5 22.hxg5 ♔e7!

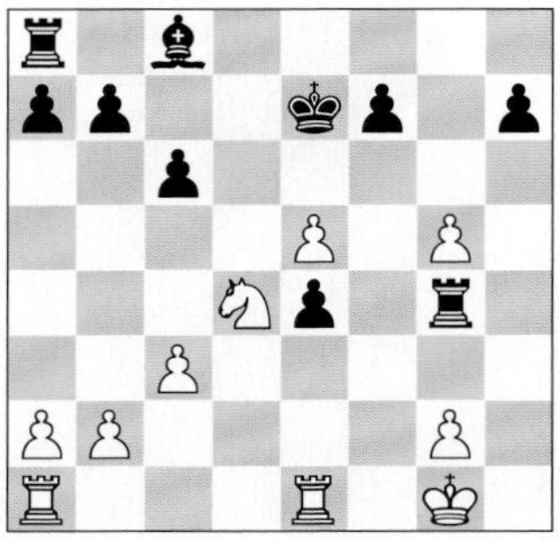

The g5-pawn is doomed, and there is no rush picking it up. ...♗d7 and ...♖ag8 are inevitable.

23.♖ad1 ♗d7! 24.e6

Desperate, Fabiano throws up a last-ditch defence, but it won't help.

24...fxe6 25.g6 hxg6

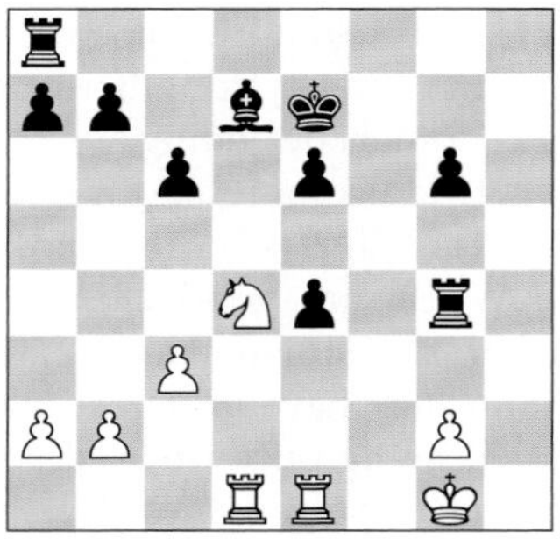

26.♘b3

I thought the point was to bring the knight to e3 and hope for some kind of fortress, but with the rooks on the board and two pawns down, this is unrealistic. Fabiano tries to regain the e4-pawn, threatening ♘c5 and ♘d2, but this won't work either. After 26.♘c2 c5 27.♘e3 ♖h4 28.♔f2, 28...♗b5 provokes c4, which would be a weakness. Black should convert such a position, slowly but surely.

26...e5

The bishop comes to the rescue with ...♗f5!, and it turns out that the b7-pawn is not hanging, because of ...♖b8xb2.

27.♘a5 ♗e6!

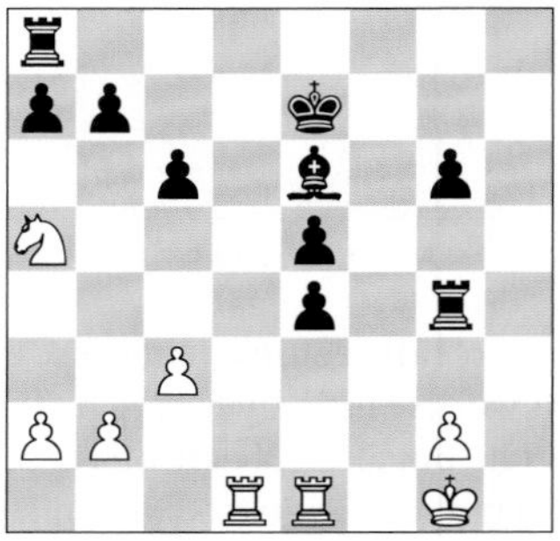

Cutting off the way back. The b7-pawn is not hanging, once again, because of ...♖b8xb2.

28.♖d2 ♖b8

The rest is easy.

29.b4 ♔f6 30.a4 ♖g3 31.♖xe4?

This loses without much resistance. 31.♖f2+ was a little tougher, but it is obviously still losing: 31...♗f5 32.♖xe4 ♔e6 33.♖c4 b6! (this is a pretty clean solution) 34.♘xc6 ♔d5!, simplifying to a technically winning endgame.

31...♗d5

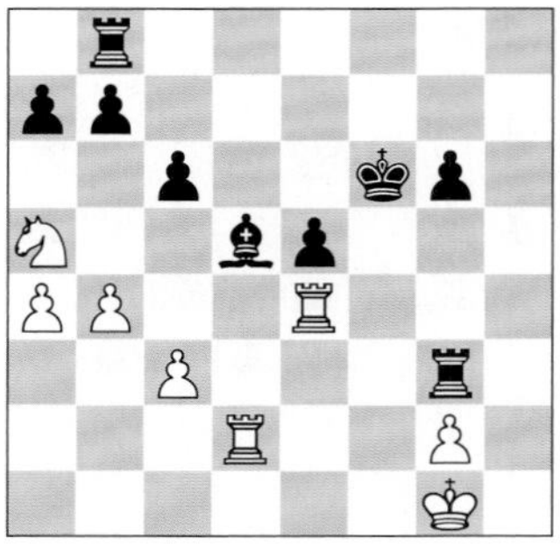

The c3-pawn will fall on the next

Bucharest 2021 **cat. XXI**

					1	2	3	4	5	6	7	8	9	10		TPR
1	Shakhriyar Mamedyarov	IGM	AZE	2770	*	1	½	½	½	½	½	1	1	½	6	2862
2	Levon Aronian	IGM	ARM	2781	0	*	½	1	½	½	1	½	½	½	5	2780
3	Wesley So	IGM	USA	2770	½	½	*	½	½	½	½	1	½	½	5	2781
4	Alexander Grischuk	IGM	RUS	2776	½	0	½	*	½	½	1	½	1	½	5	2781
5	Anish Giri	IGM	NED	2780	½	½	½	½	*	½	½	½	0	1	4½	2747
6	Teimour Radjabov	IGM	AZE	2765	½	½	½	½	½	*	½	½	½	½	4½	2749
7	Bogdan-Daniel Deac	IGM	ROU	2627	½	0	½	0	½	½	*	½	½	1	4	2731
8	Fabiano Caruana	IGM	USA	2820	0	½	0	½	½	½	½	*	1	½	4	2710
9	Constantin Lupulescu	IGM	ROU	2656	0	½	½	0	1	½	½	0	*	½	3½	2684
10	Maxime Vachier-Lagrave	IGM	FRA	2760	½	½	½	½	0	½	0	½	½	*	3½	2672

move, and the knight on a5 is completely out of play.

32.♖h4 ♖xc3 33.♖h7 b6

This allows some kind of tactical trick, but in the end Shakh converts cleanly and with some margin as well.

34.♘xc6

This doesn't quite work. White is still a pawn down, even if he wins the piece back, but Black, meanwhile, will have some time to do more damage.

34...♗xc6 35.♖c7 ♖c1+ 36.♔f2 ♖f8

There are many ways to force a winning rook ending, and what Shakh does wins as well.

37.b5 ♔e6+ 38.♔g3 ♖c3+ 39.♔h2

Shakh's body language seemed to indicate he had missed something, but after composing himself he found a clean solution.

39...♖h8+ 40.♔g1 ♖h1+!

This forces a winning rook ending.

Cristian Chirila, clearly enjoying his stay in his native Bucharest, congratulates Shakhriyar Mamedyarov on his win in the Superbet Classic.

White gets back one pawn in the end, but the king is cut off way too far.

41.♔xh1 ♗xg2+ 42.♖xg2 ♖xc7 43.♖xg6+ ♔d5

The rook ending is hopeless, and Black is threatening to gobble up the queenside pawns eventually.

44.a5 ♔c5 45.axb6 axb6 46.♖e6 ♔xb5 47.♖xe5+ ♖c5

With the king on h1, this is not even close to a draw for White.

48.♖e1 ♖g5

The king is cut off too far away and Black will push his b-pawn. The winning idea here is that Black will get ...b5, then play ...♔c5, when White will have to start giving checks: ♖c1+ ♔d4 ♖b1 ♔c3 ♖c1+ ♔b2 and ... b4 next.

■ ■ ■

Once he had completed his hattrick, Shakhriyar Mamedyarov eased down on the accelerator and comfortably drew his last two games, finishing one point ahead of his nearest rival. The winner took home $ 90,000 and the first trophy of the 2021 Grand Chess Tour. ■

Mamedyarov took home $90,000 and the first trophy of the 2021 Grand Chess Tour

Interview Sam Shankland

'I am not a believer in the rating inflation theory. I think that's nonsense. We play better today.'

Prague will always have a special place in Sam Shankland's heart. Last year, the American overcame a prolonged period of misery in the Czech capital, only to see a paralysing pandemic abruptly robbing him of the chance to follow up on his fine showing. Sixteen months he had to wait before he finally returned to the board, in the same Golden City. After his victory in the 2021 Prague Masters with a 2900 performance, Shankland spoke at length with **DIRK JAN TEN GEUZENDAM** about failures and achievements. About his successes as a chess author, and his boundless and unwavering ambitions as a player.

Great highs and deep lows – Sam Shankland knows all about them and how they can appear in droves. A glorious 2018, with triumphs in the US Championship, the Capablanca Memorial and the American Continental Championship, was followed by a year of shattered illusions and setbacks. The magnitude of his *annus horribilis* only became clear when he posted an article on Facebook after his good result in Prague last year (Shankland was part of a five-way tie for first, but Alireza Firouzja won the play-off – see New In Chess 2020/2). The post was entitled *Back on Track*, and detailed what he had been through. From bad results and severe rating loss to health problems of both his parents, from a heartbreak in his personal life to the cut flexor tendons of his left hand, an injury that left him in pain and sleeping badly for two months – he seemed to have been spared very little.

But now he was back on track. And then the pandemic brought over-the-board chess to a standstill. Seen in this light, it was only fair that Sam Shankland's first in-person tournament was the third edition of the Prague Masters, which had been moved from February, when the Czech Republic was in lockdown, to June. Or, as tournament director Petr Boleslav told him, 'Last year you found back your good form in Prague and now you just came to pick it up again.'

Physical exercise and dieting

After the tournament Shankland stayed in Prague, because it would be easier to travel to the World Cup in Sochi from there, and while he was there, we spoke on Skype. My first question was how he had spent the many months that he had been confined to his home in California.

'I had a really rough 2019, so bad that being stuck at home for a pandemic didn't really feel like a big deal. I made the best of it, did a lot of work. I did courses for Chessable, where I give a full reper-

Happy to be back in the Golden City. Sam Shankland (after the tournament with a new beard) on the world-famous Charles Bridge with Prague Castle in the background.

toire, playing 1.d4 for White, and the Semi-Slav and the Classical Sicilian for Black. That was well received and I enjoyed the process of working on it. And I worked out a lot. I've always taken physical exercise and dieting very seriously, but it's just a lot harder to do that when you're travelling a ton. I did my best and always stayed in pretty good shape, but I got really back into top physical condition, because I was able to go to the gym every day, as opposed to when I was getting onto a flight to another country every other week. For six months, the gyms were closed, but I can make my own gym. I have a weight vest that I can put on and run with, do push-ups. When I put on a 25-kilo weight vest, push-ups get pretty hard.'

In your Facebook post you wrote that real champions don't whine. They grit their teeth and try to fight back. How combative and resilient were you when normal chess life essentially came to a standstill?

'It was definitely frustrating, but at some point I realized I was getting kind of unhappy, and I decided I wanted to keep myself as busy as possible. I exercised like a fiend and kept doing normal chess training that I'd be doing during normal tournaments. The Chessable courses were also pretty demanding. And I've been working on a book, *Theoretical Rook Endgames*. Additionally, it gave me the opportunity to spend a bit more time with my parents, who live in California as well. I've had good relations with them for basically my whole life, but it's different when you don't see them very often, and now I could see them every week.'

How does working on a book or a course compare to being a professional player? Did you feel you were doing it out of necessity or does it also have an added value?

'Added value is the wrong way of putting it for the Chessable courses.

What it did is it kept me very sharp in terms of my analytical skills. There wasn't that much point in doing serious opening preparation for myself, because even in the pandemic, when there are no games, new engines come out really fast and they're getting stronger. Basically, most analysis that you are going to do is probably going to be worthless in six months. So I did very little opening work for myself, and doing these Chessable courses just kept me sharp and kept me up to date with present-day theory. And I was also able to play the analysis in the few online elite rapid events that I was invited to, which I was very happy with.'

A thing many people must be wondering about is: if a true professional is writing a book or a course on openings, how honest can they be?
'Well, I was as honest as possible. I guess the real ultimate test is, do you put your money where your mouth is and play these openings yourself? For me, at least so far, I haven't done so in classical chess, but I have in rapid. And that is basically because, while I believe that the analysis that I have presented is very strong, I also think these are not the only good lines you can play, of course. There's tons of others you can choose from. When you have that luxury of choice, choosing a line of which your analysis is out in the open, and they can just buy and look at, is probably not the best idea. But I was playing it against the best players in the world over and over again in all these rapid events and doing well, so I certainly did my best. In general, when it comes to writing, I don't write for the money. I write because it's an excuse and it forces me to study something. I write about things I want to learn about. Like when I wrote *Small Steps to Giant Improvement*, and *Small Steps II*, I wanted to learn about pawn play. So I said, OK, I am going to study this stuff and write a book. Ninety per cent of working on *Small Steps* was

'I don't write for the money. I write because it's an excuse and it forces me to study something'

finding examples and the study of it and only 10 per cent was actually writing. So it was more like I am going to do my training, and people can come along for the ride. That's what I am doing as well with *Theoretical Rook Endgames*. I have been learning rook endings really well and I hope it will be useful soon. It grows your knowledge of the game, which certainly helps. If you're going to publish something really sloppy, or on some line that you don't believe in, then you're probably not going to get a ton out of it. But if you cover some main line opening, even some that you don't have that much interest in playing, learning to play such positions helps you to develop a deeper understanding. I mean, if you're to take my Chessable work and you take the hours that I put into it, I could have used those hours perhaps more effectively if my only goal was to become a better chess player. But I don't think it would be much more in effect. I still learned a great deal from it.'

So it helps you, and it helps the people who study it. Do you believe that in general the level of chess has gone up quite dramatically over the past years?

Spot the difference. On his arrival in Prague Sam Shankland shaved off his beard.

'Yes, absolutely. I noticed actually that I had a far better score against 2200s when I was rated 2400 than when I was rated 2600. I think it's just because 2200 is stronger now than it used to be. Knowledge has increased, playing strength has increased. I am not a believer in the rating inflation theory; I think that's nonsense. We play better today. The natural progression of any sport is that the next generation will be better than the previous one.'

Controversy
There was less going on in the chess scene during the pandemic, but one of the things that happened vividly reminded me of the already mentioned Facebook post. One of the blows you took in 2019 you described as follows: 'Yet another top-10 player switched federations to the USA, probably costing me my spot on the Olympic team that I had played so well and proudly for in the past.' It was Leinier Dominguez then, now it was Levon Aronian who switched to the US Chess Federation during the pandemic. How did you receive that news?
'Obviously it was not something I was wildly thrilled about. I am going to struggle to make the team now. And I have literally had organizers write to me and say we'd love to invite you, but we already have too many US players. I look forward to more such emails. But at the end of the day, look, Aronian didn't break any rules, so I can disagree with the rules all I want, but as long as someone's following them you can't blame him. He's a very good chess player, and while on the balance it's a very negative impact for me, there's good things that can come of it, too. I get to play with him in the US Championship. He's obviously a fantastic chess player and you can learn something from that.
'In general, look, there's a reason it's controversial. I think if only good things come from something, then nobody whines and it's not a controversy. And if only bad things

'People say, don't blame the players, who make the short draws, blame the format. I've always thought you can blame the players'

come from something, it's universally condemned, so it's not a controversy either. Controversy comes when something has both positive and negative consequences. And there's no doubt there's some good that comes from it, too. I try not to think about it too much. One thing I've realized a long time ago is that I don't think there is a single political problem that you can possibly find in chess that can be solved with a hundred-grade advice. So I've just been doing my best to try to get better, and if I am 2800 in, like, a few years, then it will not particularly matter who's registered to the US. I should focus only on what I can control and not on other stuff.'

Still, the Olympiad team is clearly something special for you...
'From the moment I went to school and put my hand over my heart for the Pledge of Allegiance every day, it's always been a big dream of mine to play for my country. It's a great honour to play for my country and it's tougher when all of a sudden your spot on the team is in jeopardy. But at the end of the day, this is competition, this is sport, this is what you have to do. You can whine about the flag that a player has next to their name, or you can try to get better and beat them. If your goal is to become an elite grandmaster and become one of the absolute best players in the world, you're gonna have to play against guys like Aronian and Caruana and you will have to fight with them regardless of what country they play for. Just get over it and play; don't think about it.'

I also thought of players like you when the controversy arose about the many draws in recent tournaments, where
players silently agreed not to play at all. In that same Facebook post you wrote about 2019, 'A last minute change to the qualification rules for the FIDE Grand Prix left me stranded on the sidelines when I was counting on playing, watching in total disgust as most of the guys who did get invited made 15-move draws every other game.' Has this phenomenon become worse of late?
'Yeah, I don't want to call any particular names, but there's a few people who I feel are the big offenders. But they're starting to spread their ways to others. When they make draws every game and someone makes a draw with that person, and then they start doing it, too. In general, I think you should just invite diverse fields of players. I don't remember any short draws basically ever in Wijk aan Zee, certainly not from when I played there. As far as I know, they don't have any anti-draw rules. They're just, if you're going to make quick draws, we're not going to invite you back next year. They also invite a diverse range of players. They give some spots to players who are very good chess players, but they're not in the top-10. They may be number 20 or 30 in the world. And when there is at least some mismatch, you're going to see fewer of these quick draws as well. When you have people who have more to lose and people who have less to lose, you're going to see different levels of ambition. Generally, having a more diverse field and knowing who is a fighter and who is not is probably going to help a lot. People say, don't blame the players, who make the short draws, blame the format. They criticize this format, that format... I've always thought you can blame the players. There are players who do not do that, and I don't see why others would need to.'

Sam Shankland

1991	October 1, born in Berkeley, California, USA
2008	California State Champion
2008	3rd place in U-18 World Youth Championship
2008	International Master
2010	US Junior Champion
2011	International Grandmaster
2011	3rd place in US Championship
2012	Wins Northern Californian International
2013	Wins Dresden ZMDI Open
2014	Tromsø Olympiad gold medal on reserve board scoring 9/10
2014	Shared 1st in American Continental Championship
2016	Wins Biel Masters
2016	Baku Olympiad, Board 4 of golden US team
2018	US Champion, ahead of Caruana, So and Nakamura
2018	Wins Capablanca Memorial
2018	Wins American Continental Championship
2019	Peak rating 2731 (February)
2020	Prague Masters, 5th place after 5-way tie for first
2021	Wins Prague Masters

Hard calculation work
But now for the good news! After 16 months you returned to Prague to play a real chess tournament again. How difficult was it to travel there?
'Physically? It wasn't so hard. I stayed in Glasgow with my coach Jacob Aagaard for three weeks and did some intense training. I had already been double-vaccinated at that point. I had to have a COVID test, and then I had to take two more upon arriving in the UK. And I had to stay in his home for 10 days without leaving. There were certainly some restrictions. I wouldn't call them hard, maybe annoying is a better word. It's sort of unpleasant that you can't leave home, but it wasn't difficult.

Jacob Aagaard is not only your coach, but also your publisher and friend. How did you spend your time together?

'We didn't train as intensively as normal. There was about one week when we were doing six to seven hours of hard calculation work, which were really demanding. You can't really do that for three weeks. But we were very consistent about getting training done. And when I was there, I also did a lot of work on *Theoretical Rook Endgames*. We talked a bit about psychology, but for the most part he was just getting me back into shape during lots of calculation work. I think that's the thing you lose first when you're away from chess for a while. And that's something I think I got basically back when I was there. I calculated pretty well in Prague. I didn't calculate perfectly, I don't think you ever will, but I was reasonably satisfied with my level.'

That's also the kind of work you do with him during the year, from a distance…

'Yeah, but it doesn't work as well, it's harder to do. It doesn't feel as genuine to me. Among other things, like physically having a computer in my sight makes it feel so much less serious. And there is no other way to communicate without a computer. When I do my normal calculation with him when training, I have the board set up and he's got the computer that's turned away. I can't see the screen and I am just focusing on the board. It feels a lot more similar to a tournament game, and it's so much easier to take it seriously like that, at least for me. We did some work through the year and we tried to be as consistent as possible, but there's no replacing face-to-face training, and I was really glad we got quite a bit in before Prague.'

Does he insist on you sitting in front of a real board or is that clearly your wish?

'We both wish that, that's for sure.

I noticed, for example, that I struggled a bit in the online events, the online Olympiad, the online US Championship. I played fine, not amazingly. I just noticed that literally looking at the board was just harder. I can easily take a look at a 3-D board and superimpose a position over the board in my head based on calculating a few

'In terms of my ability to calculate, I really believe I calculate best on a 3-D board, second best blindfolded and third best on a 2-D board'

moves down the road. I just couldn't do that on 2-D. In terms of my ability to calculate, I really believe I calculate best on a 3-D board, second best blindfolded and third best on a 2-D board. I was even playing these events and looking at the ceiling and closing my eyes. So I was really happy to play on a 3-D board again.'

Before the tournament you shaved off your beard and posted a before and after photo…

'I shaved before the tournament started. I don't like shaving, just because I am lazy. It doesn't strike me as a wildly interesting thing to do, but I grow really, really fast. I hadn't actually shaved when I was at Jacob's place, so I had three weeks' real scruff. I looked like an absolute lumberjack. I shaved it all off before Prague and here I am eleven days later, you can really tell it grows pretty fast. I'll shave before the World Cup and I'll see how much beard I have when I play there.'

So there was no symbolism or superstition or anything…

'No, there isn't. At the US Championship, the year I won, I shaved before the tournament and didn't shave during the tournament. And before the last round I was like, you should not look homeless, there's a chance you might win this tournament today, so you have to shave this morning.'

Tearing apart one of the best

Your start in the Prague Masters was most encouraging. After a draw in the first round you defeated the top-seed Duda in a sharp game.

'The game with Grandelius in the first round; at some point I thought I was outplaying him, but nothing materialized and I probably should have been an adult and make a couple of solid moves and make a pretty easy draw. But I pushed a little too hard and then I was even worse. This felt like non-objective decision-making, and I was sort of wondering if I was calculating badly or if I was just kind of rusty.

'But then with Duda, who I had always a good score against in the past, I basically beat him straight out of the opening. I prepared it all the way to 22.a4, and White's winning here [you will find Sam Shankland's full notes to this game at the end of the interview – ed.]. It was a very straightforward game, and I remember going back to my room thinking I had basically, without much effort, been tearing apart one of the best players in the world. I definitely felt a lot more confident after that.'

That game won the best-game prize named after Lubosh Kavalek, who sadly died last January. Did that have special significance for you, seeing that Kavalek was born in Prague and then moved to the US, where he won the national championship three times?

'It definitely was nice to win that prize and pay homage to another US Champion. I met Kavalek only once in my life, in Prague last year. He was very friendly and very humble. I really liked the man. From one US Champion to another, that is sort of a bond you feel, or at least I do. It was a real honour to meet him, if only briefly, and to have won an award that bears his name.'

But you thought your win in the next round against David Navara was a better effort...

'Well, my game against Duda was a very good game, but most of it was high-level preparation that busted someone that strong in a main line. But it wasn't like I felt the moves I found over the board were wildly tough. While with Navara I was much happier with my play. I equalized comfortably as Black, but I started to do really a lot of work at the board and calculated well, understanding the consequences of strategic decisions while outplaying him. It was certainly a more demanding game to play at the board [the game against Navara you will also find at the end of the interview with notes by Sam Shankland – ed.].'

Things continued to go well and in Round 5 you won against Nijat Abasov, a win that took you to plus-3.

'This was the first time I thought I straight-out got lucky. Perhaps Nijat was rusty from the break, I don't know. Both this game and the final-round game against Jorden (van Foreest) I got a slightly better position that felt like risk-free pressure for White. But both of them defended well, Jorden even to the point where I was the one who had to find the only moves. On move 38 Abasov was one move from making a draw and just lost it. But it's very hard to win a strong tournament without getting lucky. I don't think I played well enough to deserve plus-4, but some extra points came.'

Kings on e4 and e5

In the last round, you defended a half-point lead over Duda and Wojtaszek, who played each other. Duda attacked and was rewarded when his fellow-countryman grabbed a poisoned pawn.

Jan-Krzysztof Duda
Radoslaw Wojtaszek
Prague Masters 2021 (7)

position after 29...♕d7

White's position looks slightly more attractive, but Black's defences should hold. Duda tries his luck with a piece sacrifice to see how vulnerable the black king is.

30.♗xh6 gxh6 31.♕g6+ ♔h8
The king could also go to f8.
32.♕xh6+ ♕h7 33.♕f6+ ♕g7 34.♕xe6
Now 34...♘e7 would have kept the black defence well-coordinated and together, but Wojtaszek defends with another knight move that leaves his king in mortal danger.
34...♘xd4? 35.♘xd4 ♕xd4 36.♕h6+ ♔g8 37.♖e8+

A rude awakening. 37...♗f8 38.♖xf8 is mate, and so is 37...♔f7 38.♕e6+ ♔g7 39.♖g8+ ♔h7 40.♕g6, mate. Black resigned.

Perseverance and not giving up feature prominently in Sam Shankland's character. A few days after our interview he sent us this selfie and quoted what he wrote on Facebook: 'In October 2018, I was in Prague for 10 days and I asked the girl at the front desk of Karlin Form Factory to go to dinner with me. She said she'd go if I made it to the top of the pegboard. I fell on the last slot and suffered a minor strain to my left arm in the process. I still vividly remember hugging the vodka bottle from the freezer as a makeshift icepack. Now two and a half years later I am back in Prague with some free time. The girl is long gone, but I finally got to face my old nemesis again. And I have to say, revenge has never tasted so sweet!'

What was the situation in your game against Van Foreest when Wojtaszek resigned?

'Actually this was funny. I don't know what happened, but somehow the way the kings ended up on the board after the Duda-Wojtaszek game I believed that it had ended in a draw. I saw the kings on e4 and e5 [the way the arbiter places the kings on electronic boards to indicate a draw – ed.] and didn't realize that Duda had won. At this point, I had been slightly better against Jorden for the whole game and the only question was if I could turn this into something tangible. I saw a few lines that should lead to a rook ending a pawn up that should be a draw. I was sort of dissatisfied with those. I ended up taking too many risks and I really lost control of the game.

'Right around when their game ended and I believed it was a draw, was the point where I thought, wait a minute, why didn't I stop pressing

'The way the kings ended up on the board after the Duda-Wojtaszek game I believed that it had ended in a draw'

and accept that maybe I won't win this game? Next thing I know my king is on e4, and I think, what have I done?'

Sam Shankland
Jorden van Foreest
Prague Masters 2021 (7)

position after 36.hxg5

'Here he played **36...h4** and I replied **37.gxh4** and was still confident, because I had calculated up to 43.♔e4 and didn't see a mate while being two pawns up. **37...♕g4+ 38.♔f1 ♖c8 39.♕a3 ♕d1+ 40.♔g2** Of course he could now force a draw with 40...♕g4+, but he played **40...♖c1** which is actually the best move, as it forces me to find **41.♔g3** By now

A delighted Sam Shankland with the crystal trophy for the winner of the 3rd Prague Masters.

I had more time to calculate and realized he had to go for a perpetual. **41...♕g1+ 42.♔f4 ♕h2+ 43.♔e4** Now he had to go for the perpetual with 43...♕h1+ or 43...♕xh4+, but he must have missed something and went **43...♕g2+?** I couldn't believe it and played **44.f3**

and now I knew I was winning. He played **44...♕h3** and actually offered me a draw. At this point, I thought that would just clinch me the tournament, because I thought Duda-Wojtaszek had been a draw. But I was looking and this was just so completely winning. I would not be able to look at myself in the mirror if I took a draw here.'

[The game continued 45.♕f8 ♖c8 – inviting 46.♕xc8?? ♕f5 mate – 46.♕f7 ♕xh4+ 47.♔f4 ♕xf4+ 48.♔xf4, and White won on move 62 – ed.]

The title of your Facebook post was 'Back on Track'. Do you feel you're back on track again?
'Yeah. Basically in 2018 my performance rating across the whole year was like 2770. If that year had been the only year that had been counted, if 2017 and everything before had just been wiped away, I would have been something like number 9 in the world. To go from that to 2019, where I just totally failed to overcome the challenges in my life and just totally fell apart... And then come back and have a 2900 performance, winning a tournament in dominant fashion with 57 per cent Black, that's pretty reasonable. I feel like I am playing well again, at mid-2700 level, and I hope I can get back to that level soon.

Your next tournament is the World Cup. And for the rest of the year ahead? Playing lots of more chess?

'I am certainly going to play more chess. I am going to try to live the same kind of life that I lived before the pandemic. I will still write books, but it will be very different. Writing *Theoretical Rook Endgames* over the course of a year and a half, as opposed to cracking out Chessable course after Chessable course, like it's the end of the world. In terms of content production, I predict that the frequency level will easily drop 90 per cent, but it's not going to completely disappear.'

NOTES BY
Sam Shankland

Sam Shankland
Jan-Krzysztof Duda
Prague Masters 2021 (2)
Sicilian Defence, Najdorf Variation

1.e4!
I am not much of a king's pawn player, but I did a fair amount of work on a main line 1.e4 repertoire during the break. I still would not call it my main move, but I felt confident enough to give it a try in my first white game in a long time.
1...c5 2.♘f3 d6 3.d4 cxd4 4.♘xd4 ♘f6 5.♘c3 a6 6.f3

My opponent was clearly not expecting this opening choice, as he spent ten minutes here deciding which variation to play.
6...e5 7.♘b3 ♗e6 8.♗e3

8...♗e7 The first surprise. I had only ever seen Duda play 8...h5 before, which is the modern main move. I had prepared some interesting ideas and probably could have put him under some pressure, but in hindsight, I'm sure he regretted not sticking to his guns.
9.♕d2 0-0 10.0-0-0 ♘bd7 11.g4 b5 12.g5
This straightforward English Attack used to be the absolute main line of the Najdorf, but in recent years, both sides have been deviating a little bit. The nuanced 12.♖g1 is also very common, but I was in a much more direct mood.

12...b4?
The question mark is there only for this move's practical value. While I believe Black is objectively okay here, the positions are absurdly sharp, very forcing, and can often be irrational. The best moves are very hard for humans to find, and the game is much more about memorization of long computer lines. When considering my opponent's big think on move 6 and his critical error a few moves later, I would be shocked if Duda had checked this line anytime recently.

12...♘h5 is a fully playable alternative, and a much safer one for Black if he is caught unprepared. There is still a lot of imbalance and interesting play left, for example after 13.♘d5 ♗xd5 14.exd5 when White is ready for a quick ♘a5-c6 and then eventually ♔b1, ♖c1, and c4. But Black has good counterplay with 14...f6!, when he takes the fight to White on the kingside. The positions are very rich and unbalanced, but they are not so sharp that one mistake tends to be decisive. Under the circumstances, I think Jan-Krzysztof would have been well advised to aim for a position like this one.
13.♘e2 ♘e8 14.f4 a5 15.f5 The play is taking on a very forcing nature.
15...a4

16.fxe6! The modern main line.
16.♘bd4 was the old main move a long time ago, but it has fallen out of favour ever since Anand's brilliant double piece sacrifice against Karjakin (Wijk aan Zee 2006). If you have not seen this game, I urge you to look it up immediately!
16...axb3 17.cxb3! fxe6 18.♗h3

While I believe 12...b4 was a poor decision based on the circumstances, it is only here that Duda made his first objective mistake, but in my opinion, it is already a decisive one. This is a very unforgiving position to play if you're caught unprepared.

18...♘c7? Tempting as it may be to save the e6-pawn, this move leaves Black with a more or less lost position. Once White saves a2, Black will have no counterplay whatsoever, and a lot of his pawns will be very vulnerable to harassment.

Good or bad, 18...♖xa2! absolutely has to be played. Black still has some work to do after 19.♗xe6+ ♔h8 20.♘g3, with ♖hf1 coming next, but he should

20.exd5! exd5 21.♗g2!

The rook is now forced to the unfortunate a5-square.

21...♖a5 22.a4!

I knew I would still need to be accurate, but I was also aware that in my opening analysis I had concluded the position is objectively won

be able to hang on with precise play.

19.♔b1 It's already a real pain to protect the b4-pawn.

19...d5 A natural move, but I was still prepared. The tempting 19...♕b8? is met with a powerful response: 20.♗xe6+! ♘xe6 21.♕d5, when White gets his piece back and is completely winning, with an extra pawn and a dominant position.

After 19...♖b8 White prevents the ...d5 break with 20.♗g2! and can look for h4 and ♖c1 next to put further pressure on Black's position. Optically, it might not seem all that bad, but the computer claims Black is already dead lost.

The pawn is immune from capture, and White is completely winning. He has easy play against Black's centre pawns, with moves like ♖h1-e1 and ♘c1-d3 on the way. He can gain further space with h2-h4 and even reroute the bishop back to h2 via g1. Eventually, the centre will crumble. Black has no real counterplay, his pieces do not have secure squares to try to keep the pawns protected, and most importantly, White is always ready to meet ...d5-d4 with ♘e2xd4. I knew I would still need to be accurate, but I was also aware that in my opening analysis I had concluded the position is objectively won.

22...♔h8 The first new move of the game for me, but it was hardly an intimidating one. I figured that Black's idea was that he wanted to push ...d4 next without letting me sacrifice, but this was not too hard to prevent.

Some correspondence games went 22...♖f7, but Black's position will not be saved. For example, after 23.♖he1 ♗f8 24.h4 d4 25.♘xd4 exd4 26.♕xd4 Black's position is collapsing.

And after 22...d4? 23.♘xd4 exd4 24.♕xd4 White will soon win his piece back, because the knight on d7 cannot move: 24...♘c5 (24...♘e5 25.♕b6, and everything is hanging) 25.♕c4+!. Check, and the queen is hanging. I believe this was the position Duda was considering, and this is why he chose to play 22...♔h8.

23.♖he1

I spent some 20 minutes on this move, which might not have been entirely necessary, but I am glad that I did. I wanted to calculate very closely to make sure that ...d4 would not come, and once I was satisfied, I knew bringing my rooks to the centre had to be right.

23...♖a6

This is not a subtle move. Black clearly wants to bring his rook to d6 to help force through ...d4 at a moment when I cannot take it. This is sensible enough, but it is very slow and it allows White to regroup his pieces very effectively.

The position after 23...d4 24.♘xd4! exd4 25.♕xd4 ♘c5 is not as straightforward for White as it would be with the king back on g8, but I still was able to calculate it out to a win: 26.♕xb4 ♘7a6 27.♕c3 (according to the machine, 27.♕c4, with ♗e3-d2 to come next, is even stronger, but my plan during the game was to put the queen on c3) 27...♕b6 28.♗d4!, and Black is facing too many threats, and something will fall.

24.h4! Overprotecting g5.
24...♖d6

25.♗g1! So that now this move becomes possible. White is ready for ♘c1-d3 and ♗g1-h2, when Black will be unable to hold his centre together.
25...h6 This is probably the best move under the circumstances, trying to introduce some complications in another part of the board at all cost, but it will not save Black.
I was expecting 25...♗e6, but that will not save Black either: 26.♗h3 ♘ec5 27.♘c1, and Black can no longer maintain the centre. Something will fall.
26.♕xb4! There are no discoveries to be scared of, and attacking the rook on d6 means that Black will not be able to take twice on g5.
26...d4 Or 26...♖b6 27.♕c3 d4 28.♘xd4 exd4 29.♗xd4, and Black is done for.

Jan-Krzysztof Duda is always spoiling for a sharp fight, but this time he got lost in a labyrinth where his opponent had a compass.

27.♘c1!
A typical theme I was aware of when studying the position with the machine before the game. The knight will be much better placed on d3.
27...♘d5

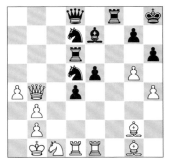

28.♕b5
My original plan was 28.♗xd5, and it is probably good enough, but I ultimately decided I would rather trade my bishop for the d7-knight instead, as this will undermine the e5-pawn: 28...♖xd5 29.♕c4 ♘b6 30.♕c2, and with ♘d3 coming next, White should win.

28...♘f4 29.♗c6!
Now Black will struggle to defend the e5-pawn.
29...hxg5 30.hxg5

30...♘b8
After 30...♗xg5 White has other good moves, but 31.♗xd7 is by far the simplest. As soon as e5 falls, the game is over: 31...♖d5 32.♕c6 ♖f6 33.♕c8! (after this final important move, Black will be unable to recapture his lost piece without losing e5 in the process) 33...♖xd7 34.♕xd8+ ♖xd8 35.♖xe5, and it's time to resign.
31.♗e4 ♘d7
I spent some time here trying to make ♗xd4 work to give mate on the h-file, but ultimately did not manage to do so and found a simpler solution.

32.g6! Now, if the g6-pawn stays alive, Black's king will be in terrible danger. But it turns out to be very hard to capture.
32...♖b6
32...♘xg6 33.♗xd4! exd4 34.♕h5+, and White wins.
33.♕c4 ♘xg6
Now that the knight has left f4, I can complete my own knight's regrouping.

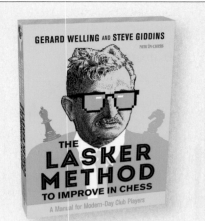
34.♘d3 ♘f4 35.♗c6!

Back to c6, and this time ...♘b8 is not a thing anymore. Additionally, the rook on c6 is now cut off, in danger of being harassed with a4-a5, and unable to block a check on the h-file.

35...♗h4

Anything wins here, but I saw the chance to take the e5-pawn, and even at the cost of an exchange I did not have to be asked twice.

35...♘b8 is met by 36.♘xe5!.

35...♘xd3 certainly won't save Black. After 36.♖xd3 ♘b8 White is winning every which way, but I had calculated an amusing variation during the game. Checks and captures all the way through: 37.♖h3+ ♗h4 38.♖xe5 ♖xc6 39.♖h5+ ♖h6 40.♖xh6+ gxh6 41.♗xd4+ ♗f6 42.♖xh6+ ♔g7 43.♖xf6 ♖xf6 44.♗xf6+! ♕xf6 (44...♔xf6 45.♕h4+) 45.♕c7+, and White ends up with three extra pawns in the queen ending.

36.♖xe5!

36...♘xe5

36...♘xd3 37.♖h5 is a nice checkmate.

37.♘xe5 ♕f6 38.♗xd4 ♖bb8 39.♘d7

Black resigned. The final position is a very painful one for him.

NOTES BY Sam Shankland

**David Navara
Sam Shankland**
Prague Masters 2021 (3)
English Opening, Four Knights Variation

Coming into the third round, David Navara was already having a very rough tournament, losing his first two games. But he had played Black in both of them, and I knew that he would be coming for blood in his first chance to make the opening move.

1.c4 e5

I have not chosen this move much before, but I had decided that adding c4 e5 to my repertoire would be a good idea. With sixteen months off, I had ample time to make it happen.

2.♘c3 ♘f6 3.♘f3 ♘c6 4.g3 d5 5.cxd5 ♘xd5 6.♗g2

6...♗c5!? I quite like this move, which has become a hot trend in the last couple of years. In my opinion, the bishop is actually not that great on this diagonal, and I was quite happy to tuck it back away on f8 once I had castled, but the main point is that its placement on c5 means that Black need not burn a tempo on moving his d5-knight again. Strategically, 6...♗e7? is a better square for the bishop, but tactically it does not work out: 7.♘xe5! ♘xc3 8.♗xc6+ bxc6 9.dxc3, and White is a clean pawn up. It helps a lot that after 9...♕xd1+ 10.♔xd1 the pawn on f2 is not hanging!

7.0-0 Obviously, 7.♘xe5 is critical, but it also highlights why the bishop is better on c5. After 7...♘xc3 8.♗xc6+ bxc6 9.dxc3 ♕xd1+ 10.♔xd1 ♗xf2! Black grabs back a very critical pawn and has a fine position.
7...0-0 8.d3 ♖e8 9.♗g5 For better or for worse, this is the main move, but it really does not make much sense to me. I think Black is happy enough to play ...f6, to bolster the centre while it is not weakening enough to justify White losing two tempi.
9...♘xc3 10.bxc3 f6 11.♗c1 ♗e6 12.♗b2 Now, it seems like White is ready for d4.
12...♗f8!

As mentioned before, I think the bishop is not well placed on the g1-a7 diagonal, and that it only went there for concrete reasons. I like this move much more than putting it back on b6.
13.♕c2
13.d4 is possible, but not too threatening: 13...exd4 14.cxd4 (14.♘xd4? ♗d5) 14...♗d5. Black has neutralized the long diagonal and White's centre will advance no further. This is exactly the kind of position I had in mind when I thought the bishop would be better on f8 than on b6. After 15.e3 ♘a5 Black is ready for ...c5 next, and he looks quite fine to me.

I knew that David Navara would be coming for blood in his first chance to make the opening move

13...♕d7 14.♖fd1 ♕f7!
I was already thinking about 14...♘a5, aiming to fight for control of the c4-square as prophylaxis against d3-d4, but it makes a lot less sense here. After 15.♘d2 White is ready for c4 and ♗c3, when he looks pretty comfortable to me.

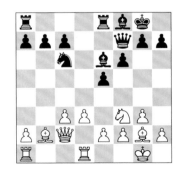

15.e4?
The first big mistake. White had to take this one last chance to play d4 under decent circumstances.
After 15.d4!, Black is not in time to

get his knight to a5 and c4. Still, he is quite fine in more ways than one. During the game, my plan was to take: 15...exd4 16.♘xd4 ♗c4 17.♘xc6 ♖xe2 18.♕a4 bxc6 19.♗xc6 ♖b8, and I would expect a draw pretty soon. The position will liquidate.
15...♘a5!

I really like this move. Black anticipates d4 coming, and is ready to abuse the weakened c4-square in the resulting structure. It only makes sense to play it now that White has committed to e2-e4.
16.♘d2
16.c4 would be a typical response if Black played ...♘a5 with the pawn still on e2. Then, ♘d2 and ♗c3 might follow. But here, the pawn on e4 totally ruins White's position.
After 16.d4 ♘c4 White's central advance has not done much for him, the knight on c4 is a monster, and the bishop on b2 is really bad, a theme we will continue to see for the rest of the game. After 17.d5 ♗d7, ...c7-c6 is coming, and Black looks better to me, playing against White's centre in a somewhat Grünfeld-esque style.
16...♖ad8
According to the machines, the natural 16...c5 is best. It makes a lot of sense to prevent d4 forcefully and gain a lot of space, but I was worried about 17.♘f1, when White's knight will soon reach d5. The computers find this plan a lot less annoying than I did during the game.
17.d4 c6!
Just stopping d4-d5. Despite the big centre, White's position looks very difficult to me. He has no real plan,

and it is very hard for him to move any of his pieces. Moving the knight will allow ...♞c4. The bishop on b2 cannot move without dropping the d4-pawn. The rook on a1 is stuck defending a2. In the meantime, Black is super-solid and can look for any number of plans next, the most natural of which would be ...♜d7 and ...♜ed8.

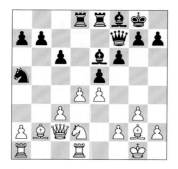

After a long think, David decided to drastically change the nature of the position.

18.f4!

White is still in big trouble, but I do think this is the best move. He had to do something dramatic.

18...exf4!?

This is not the only good move, but a very direct one. Black changes the pawn structure.

The machine is quite happy to maintain the status quo with 18...♛c7 and claims that Black is much better here. But I saw another tempting option.

19.gxf4 f5! 20.e5 c5!

If White was able to advance d4-d5, he should win the game immediately, but Black has enough pieces fighting for the d5-square that this should never happen. Additionally, the ...c5 advance pressures the d4-pawn, making c3-c4 nothing but a pipe dream.

21.♞f3?

This is the wrong place for the knight to go. It is now a long way from fighting for the c4- and d5-squares. Best was 21.♞f1!, which is what I was expecting during the game. After 21...♞c4 22.♜d3 White can play ♜a1-d1 next. Once the rook is no longer in the corner, he can fix the bishop with ♝b2-c1, and eventually play for ♞f1-e3. I still think he is worse, but the game goes on.

21...♝e7 22.♚h1 ♞c4 23.♛e2

♛h5 24.a4

This was the last tough strategic decision of the game. After 24.d5? ♜xd5! the tactics favour Black.

24...♞b6! I really like this move. The knight on c4 looked nice, but was not doing that much. Now, it can look for greener pastures on d5.

25.dxc5 I had considered the position after 25.a5 ♞d5 26.♛d2 c4 and decided Black should be winning. He has locked the position up completely, blockaded the two central pawns on a permanent basis, and can slowly but surely break on either or both sides of the board with ...b7-b5-b4 or ...g7-g6 and ...g7-g5.

25...♝xc5

David was in massive time-trouble here, which should explain the next oversight, but there are already no good moves. The machine is recommending c3-c4, when Black can even choose which pawn he wants to take.

26.♛b5? This makes some sense, unpinning the f3-knight with a gain of tempo to get ready for something like ♞g5, but I was ready for it. After 26.c4 ♜xd1+ 27.♜xd1 ♞xa4 Black should win.

Prague Masters 2021												cat. XVIII
				1	2	3	4	5	6	7	8	TPR
1 Sam Shankland	IGM	USA	2691	*	1	½	½	1	½	1	1	5½	2905
2 Jan-Krzysztof Duda	IGM	POL	2729	0	*	1	½	½	1	1	1	5	2827
3 Radoslaw Wojtaszek	IGM	POL	2687	½	0	*	½	1	½	½	1	4	2725
4 Nguyen Thai Dai Van	IGM	CZE	2577	½	½	½	*	½	½	½	½	3½	2691
5 Nijat Abasov	IGM	AZE	2665	0	½	0	½	*	1	½	1	3½	2678
6 Nils Grandelius	IGM	SWE	2670	½	0	½	½	0	*	½	½	2½	2576
7 Jorden van Foreest	IGM	NED	2701	0	0	½	½	½	½	*	½	2½	2571
8 David Navara	IGM	CZE	2697	0	0	0	½	0	½	½	*	1½	2444

26...♗e3! The pawn on f4 can hardly be protected, and once it is captured, the mating threats on h2 will force the f3-knight to stay in place.

27.♖xd8 ♖xd8 28.a5 ♘c4 29.a6

Now I probably could have won in an easier way than I did, but from here I calculated a line that I was confident would win the game, and did not think beyond that.

29...bxa6 30.♕xa6 ♗d5 31.♖d1

It looks as if White is getting some counterplay, but the d-file can be clogged.

31...♗d2! Now, Black is threatening to take f3 with either piece.

31...♘d2 works, too, though I had somehow missed that after 32.♕e2 ♘xf3 33.♖xd5 I don't need to resign, and can instead give mate on h2.

32.♗c1

The most resilient, but I had already figured out what to do.

32...♔h8! Getting ready to take on f3 next without allowing ♕xc4 to come with check.

After 32...♗xf3?, 33.♕xc4+ is check! After 33...♔h8 34.♖xd2 Black can resign.

David Navara had a rough time in his home city of Prague, but true to his style the Czech number one remained ambitious in each and every game.

33.♖xd2 After 33.♗xd2 ♗xf3 White loses decisive material, thanks in no part to the move 34.♕xc4 not coming with check: 34...♗xg2+ 35.♔xg2 ♕xd1, and wins.

33...♘xd2

34.♕a5

This forces Black to find one final good move, but then it's all over. 34.♘xd2 would have made me work a little harder, but Black is surely winning after 34...♗xg2+ 35.♔xg2 ♕g4+!, when White cannot go back to h1 and must instead step to the f-file, which will involve losing all of his pawns: 36.♔f2 ♕xf4+ 37.♔g2 ♕g4+!. With a series of checks, Black gets ready to bring his queen to e1: 38.♔f2 ♕h4+ 39.♔g2 ♕e1! 40.♕f1 ♕xe5

White will lose the c3-pawn as well, and with three pawns and a rook for two pieces plus a much safer king, Black should win with no further discussion.

34...♖d7

While playing 35.♗xd2, David lost on time. If White were to try 35.♕b5 instead, Black can play 35...♘xf3, and he can block with the bishop on g8. ∎

Armageddon game decides FTX Crypto Cup

Magnus Carlsen finally gets the better of Wesley So in a Champions Tour Final

The final tiebreak match of the online FTX Crypto Cup was punctuated by outbursts of raw emotion from the World Champion. When Wesley So resigned the final Armageddon game, Magnus Carlsen roared with delight and pumped his fists ecstatically. He described his victory as 'a massive, massive relief'. **LUKE MCSHANE** reports.

Magnus Carlsen's utter relief was fully understandable. After losing to So in the Finals of the Skilling Open (in November) and the Opera Euro Rapid (in February), it would have been simply unbearable to lose a third time. This time it was all the more impressive, since Wesley So seemed to be enjoying such a smooth ride through the tournament, while nothing had come easily for the World Champion. During the first blitz game of the tiebreak, Carlsen slammed the table in disgust. Who wouldn't have felt the same way, after letting this happen in such a crucial game? He had stepped on a rake and bloodied his own nose.

Magnus Carlsen
Wesley So
CCT FTX Crypto Cup 2021 (final 3.1)

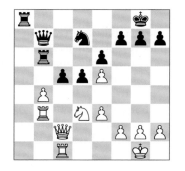

position after 25...c5!?

A wonderful trick from Wesley So. Carlsen's rush to snatch the pawn calls to mind his tongue-in-cheek claim from an interview a couple of years ago: 'My opponent is an idiot till proven otherwise.' Just occasionally, the opponent is right!
26.♘xc5 26.bxc5 ♖xb3 27.c6 ♕b6 28.cxd7 ♖d8 is not easy to judge, but is certainly better than what occurred in the game.
26...♘xc5 27.♕xc5
27.♖c3! was actually the simplest path to equality. 27...♘d7 prepares the cover the back rank with ...♘f8, but 28.♖c7 ♕b8 29.♖xd7 ♖xb4 is drawn.
27...♖c6!

28.♖bc3 ♖xc5 29.♖xc5
Carlsen staggered on for ten moves and resigned.
29...h5 30.b5 ♖a5 31.h3 g6 32.♖b1 ♔g7 33.h4 ♕b8 34.g3 ♕xe5 35.♖cc1 ♖a2 36.b6 ♕f5 37.♖f1 ♖xf2 38.b7 ♖xf1+ 39.♖xf1 ♕e5
White resigned.

Yes, there's no denying, he won. Magnus Carlsen roars with delight as he defeats Wesley So in the Armageddon game.

Fluctuating prize fund

The sixth leg of the Meltwater Champions Tour was sponsored by FTX Crypto, a cryptocurrency exchange, who added an unusual twist to the prize fund. The headline pot was $320,000, split between $220,000 in cash and 2.1825 bitcoins. The latter was valued at $100,000 before the tournament began.

The fluctuations in bitcoin's value are common knowledge, and by the end of the tournament those bitcoins had depreciated in value to around $85,000.

Still, currency transactions are a familiar hazard for travelling chess players. I cannot recall any, but there must surely be cases of players winning prizes in a local currency that had sharply depreciated before they were awarded. Bitcoin may be volatile too, but some players in history might have welcomed its utility in crossing borders.

Long ago, Rubinstein is said to have had most of his winnings impounded by Austrian border guards after his victory in Vienna, 1922. A more recent story (reported in the *New York Times*) concerns Grandmaster

Carlsen slammed the table in disgust. Who wouldn't have felt the same way, in such a crucial game?

Guillermo Garcia, who won a significant prize at the New York Open in 1988, but was legally barred from taking it home to his native Cuba.

Preliminaries

As has been the case in the last few events of the Champions Chess Tour, the preliminary stage featured sixteen players, battling it out in a round-robin for eight knockout spots. It feels a bit like watching Wijk aan Zee on steroids, except the main intrigue occurs over the middle of the table instead of the top. The field for

this was more tightly matched than usual, including all of the classical top 10, and five more from the top 30. Argentina's Alan Pichot was the only obvious underdog, voted in by chess24 premium members.

Unsurprisingly, it was heavy going for Pichot, and a case in point was his game against Caruana. Pichot played a fine game, and missed at least one knockout in the middle, but liquidated into what looked like a safe middlegame. It must have been disheartening for him to watch problems arise in this apparently safe position, but they eventually reached the position below. In Pichot's shoes I would have fancied that the draw was within reach. Superficially it does not look especially dangerous for White, but a vicious zugzwang lurks below the surface.

Alan Pichot
Fabiano Caruana
CCT FTX Crypto Cup 2021
(prelim-9)

position after 60...♗xa1

The natural plan for White is to park the king near the a-pawn, and wait for Black's king to start munching pawns on the kingside. When it munches one pawn, another can rush up the board and deflect Black's bishop. White captures the a-pawn and secures a draw.

61.♔a4?
61.f3! was the simplest way to secure the half point. For example, 61...♗d4 62.♔c4 ♗g1 63.h3 ♗f2 64.g4 ♔f4

By my count, out of 120 games in the prelims, 15 were drawn by 'database diplomacy'

65.♔b5 ♗xf3 66.g5 and White will succeed in deflecting the bishop from the a-pawn.
61.f4+ (or first 61.♔c4) draws with considerably more difficulty. White is just in time after 61...♔g4 62.♔c4 ♗f6 63.♔d3! (63.♔d5? ♗f5! 64.♔c4 ♗d8 65.♔d3 ♗b6) 63...♗d8 64.♔d4! ♗b6+ 65.♔e4 ♗g1 66.f5 ♗xh2 67.f6 ♗xg3 68.f7 ♗d6 69.♔d5.

61...♔g4
Now White is lost, but it's still not obvious where the zugzwang is coming from...
62.♔a5 ♗d4 63.f4 ♗g1 64.♔a6 ♔f5

There it is! Imagine if Black's pawn were defended on b6 instead. White could go back and forth ♔b5-a6 with an easy draw. But with the pawn on a7, White's king can't mark time as 65.♔b7? a5! is hopeless, and 65.♔b5 allows ...♗xh2.

65.h3 ♗f2 66.h4 ♔g4
Nothing has changed, and it's time for the pawns to drop.
67.h5 ♔xh5 68.f5 ♔g5 69.g4 ♗d4 White resigned.

In fact, Caruana was the only player making his debut in this season's Champions Tour, and his convincing first place in the prelims (10/15) really ought to dispel any doubts regarding his affinity for rapid chess. But while Caruana was making it look easy,

spare a thought for one of his frustrated victims.

Caruana-Grischuk
CCT FTX Crypto Cup 2021 (prelim-12)
position after 33.a4

Caruana has a pleasant endgame, but now Grischuk makes an elementary blunder.
33...♔d6? 34.c5+
Black resigned. The bishop on a6 drops off. As Caruana himself said, 'It's easy to enjoy yourself when you're doing well.'

Caruana may have dominated the prelims, but Wesley So made it look like a walk in the park. Two hard-fought victories at the start were a fine achievement, but after that he demonstrated an extreme economy of effort. From the remaining 13 games, he notched up one more win (over Pichot), three draws with a fight, and nine(!) draws which were in well-rehearsed opening variations.
Five of those nine ended with this dreary repetition, though I will note for the connoisseurs that Black occasionally plays 8...d5 (or even more rarely 8...d6) *before* the capture on d4).
1.e4 e5 2.♘f3 ♘c6 3.♗b5 ♘f6 4.0-0 ♘xe4 5.d4 ♘d6 6.dxe5 ♘xb5 7.a4 ♘bd4 8.♘xd4 ♘xd4 9.♕xd4 d5 10.exd6 ♕xd6 11.♕e4+ ♕e6 12.♕d4 ♕d6 13.♕e4+ ♕e6 14.♕d4 ♕d6.

CCT FTX Crypto Cup 2021 (prelims)

			elo rapid		TPR
1	Caruana	USA	2773	10	2880
2	Giri	NED	2731	9	2837
3	Nakamura	USA	2829	9	2831
4	Vachier-Lagrave	FRA	2860	9	2829
5	So	USA	2741	9	2837
6	Carlsen	NOR	2881	8½	2798
7	Radjabov	AZE	2758	8½	2807
8	Nepomniachtchi	RUS	2778	8	2783
9	Aronian	ARM	2778	8	2783
10	Mamedyarov	AZE	2761	7½	2766
11	Firouzja	FID	2703	7	2752
12	Svidler	RUS	2742	7	2750
13	Ding Liren	CHN	2836	7	2743
14	Dubov	RUS	2770	6	2697
15	Grischuk	RUS	2784	5	2651
16	Pichot	ARG	2533	1½	2424

When this occurs in the preliminary stage, where the structure of the event dictates that qualification is the main goal, it seems misguided to blame the players. In theory, finishing at the top of the table confers a seeding advantage in the knockout, since number 1 plays number 8, and so on. In practice, all eight qualifiers tend to be closely matched, so there is little to be gained from overexertion. Moreover, it's clear that the tournament as a whole places a heavy burden on the players' nerves, so conserving energy is a pragmatic course of action. It would be nice to tweak the format to disincentivize these draws, but that's easier said than done, since the existing format has the advantage of being easy to understand. By my count, out of 120 games in the prelims, 15 were drawn by 'database diplomacy', which strikes me as mildly disappointing but not egregious.

The Orangutan as a tonic

While So was cruising into the knockouts, Carlsen was scrambling. Sometimes, when one feels in poor form, an offbeat opening can act as a restorative tonic. Being forced to think on the spot and solve fresh problems can be just what you need. Perhaps that was on Carlsen's mind when he chose 1.b4 against Giri (the Orangutan, in my lexicon, but the Sokolsky to others). After 1.b4 e5 2.♗b2 ♗xb4 3.♗xe5 ♘f6, I was curious to see what Carlsen would do next. Etched in my mind (and a painful memory for Carlsen too,

I imagine) is a game with similar contours: Kramnik-Carlsen, Moscow Botvinnik Memorial 2011. Kramnik showed that trading the centre pawn for the wing pawn is surprisingly desirable. He stuck all his pieces in the centre and then crashed through on the kingside.

Vladimir Kramnik
Magnus Carlsen
Moscow rapid 2011
Réti Opening

1.♘f3 b5 2.e4 ♗b7 3.♗xb5 ♗xe4
4.0-0 ♘f6 5.d4 e6 6.c4 ♗e7
7.♘c3 ♗b7 8.d5 0-0 9.♗f4 ♘a6
10.♖e1

Hyper-modernism be damned. This game is a fine advert for shoving all the pieces in the centre.
**10...♕c8 11.♘d4 ♗b4 12.♗g5
♘e8 13.♖e3**

Simple chess, lifting the rook toward the newly exposed kingside.
13...c6 14.♗xa6 ♗xa6 15.♕h5
This works out perfectly in the game, but it was more precise to play 15.♖h3 first.
15...f6 After this, White's attack is too strong. The best defence was one

that looks hideous: 15...g6 16.♕h4 f6 17.♗h6 ♖f7 offers surprising resources, e.g. 18.dxe6 dxe6 19.♘xe6 ♘d6, with counterplay.

16.♖h3 fxg5

16...h6 loses in straightforward fashion: 17.♗xh6 gxh6 18.♕xh6 ♔f7 19.♕h7+ ♘g7 20.♖g3 ♖g8 21.♘e4 and there are too many threats.

17.♕xh7+ ♔f7 18.♕h5+ ♔g8 19.♕h7+ ♔f7 20.♘e4

There's no direct mate, but White's compensation is overwhelming.

20... ♗xc4 21.♕h5+ ♔e7 22.♕xg5+ ♔f7 After 22...♘f6 23.♖h7! is simplest. **23.♕h5+ ♔e7 24.♕g5+ ♔f7 25.dxe6+ dxe6**

26.♘f3! An elegant retreat to prepare ♘e5+. **26...♔g8 27.♕h4 ♖xf3 28.♕h7+** Black resigned.

Returning to Carlsen-Giri, FTX Crypto Cup prelims 2021, after the opening moves 1.b4 e5 2.♗b2 ♗xb4 3.♗xe5 ♘f6, Carlsen's concept was a surprise for me: 4.c3!? ♗e7 5.g3 (later in the event, Carlsen chose 5.e3!? against Nakamura, with similar ideas) 5...d6 6.♗xf6 ♗xf6 7.♗g2 0-0 8.e3 d5 9.♘e2 c6 10.d4 ♗f5 11.♘d2

♘d7 12.0-0 ♖e8 13.c4 dxc4 14.♘xc4.

White has achieved some sort of turbocharged Trompowsky. Carlsen later won a pawn, but the game was drawn when he failed to make anything of a very pleasant endgame.

The Baby-Orangutan

But even a struggling Carlsen can sometimes make chess look easy. A couple of rounds later, his 1.b3 did bring him a nice win in a game against Alexander Grischuk, who at that point was on just 1½/7.

NOTES BY
Peter Heine Nielsen

**Magnus Carlsen
Alexander Grischuk**
CCT FTX Crypto Cup 2021 (prelim-8)
Nimzowitsch-Larsen Attack

1.b3!?
The Baby-Orangutan, as Bent Larsen once jokingly named it, because it is just half a real Orangutan step! The good thing with these online events is that they give players the chance to play numerous first moves on the same day. In an earlier round, Magnus played the real thing and went 1.b4!? against Anish Giri. He got a winning position but got held to a draw by the Dutchman's stubborn defence. Here, however, Carlsen plays the Larsen-Nimzowitsch opening, paying a nice tribute to his coach's home-country on his birthday.
1...e5 2.♗b2 ♘c6

CHESS GOES CRYPTO

YOU LOST, BUT ELON MUSK TWEETED THAT YOU WERE WINNING...

EH, BEFORE THE GAME HE TWEETED THAT I SHOULD SACRIFICE THREE PIECES...

BEREND VONK

VONK

Funnily, both players seemed surprised that the queen had nowhere to go, when Magnus Carlsen caught Alexander Grischuk's queen in the middle of the board.

3.c4!? 3.e3 used to be the main line here, because the text has had a question mark after it after Larsen's famed Board 1 loss to Boris Spassky in just 17 moves at the 1970 Soviet Union vs. the World match in Belgrade. In that match, Larsen came back strongly, scoring 2½/4, but it took 50 years for the line to be reviewed, with Adhiban being a tireless advocate.
3...♘f6 4.♘f3 e4 5.♘d4 ♗c5

6.♘f5! Larsen used common sense, and exchanged on c6: 6.♘xc6 dxc6

7.e3 ♗f5 8.♕c2 ♕e7 9.♗e2 0-0-0 would not have hurt White if he had gone, for example, 10.a3, but after 10.f4?? ♘g4! Larsen was dead-lost [the game ended after 11.g3 h5 12.h3 h4 13.hxg4 hxg3 14.♖g1 ♖h1! 15.♖xh1 g2 16.♖f1 ♕h4+ 17.♔d1 gxf1♕+ 0-1 – ed.]. Since he had famously claimed Board 1 in the Rest-of-the-World team ahead of Bobby Fischer, this was obviously a nightmare start, but as mentioned he somehow managed to pull himself together and ended on a plus-score, beating Spassky and Leonid Stein in the process. In this game, however, White seems happy to send his knight on a fool's errand.

6...d5!? Grischuk probably knew that the engines suggest this move, and as always was ready for a principled fight. The game Adhiban-Navara from the prestigious Mr. Dodgy Invitational continued 6...0-0 7.e3 d5 8.cxd5

♘xd5?? 9.♕g4, and although Black might rightfully say that he had only played sensible developing moves, while White seemed to run rough-shod over numerous principles, the game would have ended in mate. 9...g6 10.♘h6 is mate, so Navara resigned!
7.♘xg7+ ♔f8 8.cxd5 ♗d4 9.♘c3

9...♘e7? Grischuk thought for a while here, probably trying to recreate what the computer had shown him. 9...♘b4! was the correct response, when after 10.♘h5! ♘xh5 11.e3 a complex position arises, 'awaiting further practical tests', as they used to write in the pre-computer era.
10.e3 ♗xc3 11.dxc3 ♔xg7 12.c4

Black does have an extra piece, but White has played 1.b3 for a reason, and his bishop now dominates to such an extent that the computers call White's advantage utterly winning.
12...♘g6 13.g4?! Here 13.♕d4! was even better, since the text allows 13...♔f8!, trying to evacuate, when White is still far better, but Black can at least fight. After Black's reply this is no longer a real option.
13...h6 14.h4 c5 15.♗e2 ♔g8 16.♕c2 ♖h7 17.0-0-0 ♘xg4

With ♖dg1 and g5 coming next, Grischuk stops the threat of g5 by eliminating the white pawn. Logical, but it does have the major drawback of opening lines towards his own king.

18.h5 ♘f8 19.♕xe4 f5 20.♕c2

20...♘xf2 Again not caring to wait for White to prepare his final assault, Grischuk makes things more concrete.
21.♖hg1+ ♔f7 22.♖df1 ♕h4 23.♗e5

23...♕e4?! Black's last chance was 23...♕e7, although the white queen can then alight on the bishop's initial developing square, and after 24.♕b2!? White is still winning.
24.♕c3 ♘h3 25.♖g4! Using the pin on the f-file to trap Black's queen. Grischuk resigned.

■ ■ ■

Going into the final round with a +1 score, the World Champion squeaked through into the knockouts with a win against Teimour Radjabov, who was already comfortably qualified.

Another player who was finding things tough was Ian Nepomniachtchi. He booked his knockout spot after a wild final game with Grischuk, and thanked his lucky stars that Anish Giri had taken a draw against him in a winning position two rounds earlier.

Knockouts
If the comfort levels of Carlsen and So had begun to diverge in the prelims, they seemed to grow even further apart in the knockouts. Carlsen faced Hikaru Nakamura in the quarter final, whom he had (flatteringly) described as the 'most annoying' player in the tournament, citing Nakamura's resilience in almost any position. (Indeed, Nakamura survived a grotesque position during their game from the prelims.) Their knockout match saw Carlsen on the back foot yet again, trailing three times in the rapid matches and fighting back each time, finally asserting himself during the blitz tiebreak.
Wesley So dispatched Maxime Vachier-Lagrave in the quarter final, winning both mini-matches convincingly. In the semi-final he achieved the same feat against Ian Nepomniachtchi, though rather less convincingly.

Wesley So – Ian Nepomniachtchi
FTX Crypto Cup 2021 (sf 1.3)
position after 46...♖a7

Carlsen described Hikaru Nakamura (flatteringly) as the 'most annoying' player in the tournament

Could So have had a more favourable omen than seeing his howler 46.♔b4-c3??, answered by 46...♖e7 instead of 46...♖a3+ winning the knight? The game was eventually drawn.

The next game brought more joy for Wesley, and more grief for his opponent. One might imagine that it's impossible to win a position like this one against Nepomniachtchi.

Ian Nepomniachtchi
Wesley So
CCT FTX Crypto Cup 2021 (sf 1.4)

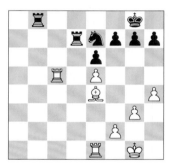

position after 28...♖c7

29.h5 g6 30.♔g2 ♔g7 31.♖h1 ♘g8 32.♖hc1 gxh5 33.♖h1 ♖b4 34.♗c2 ♘h6 35.♗d1 h4 36.♗e2 ♘e7 37.♖xh4+ ♖xh4 38.gxh4 ♘g6 39.♔g3 ♖d4 40.♖c4 ♖xc4 41.♗xc4 ♘xe5 42.♗b3 ♔g7 43.f4 ♘c6 44.♗c2 h6 45.♗b1 ♘e7 46.♔g4 ♘d5 47.♔g3 ♔f8 48.♔g4 ♘f6+ 49.♔f3 ♔e7 50.♗c2 ♘h5 51.♔g4 ♘g7

It looks unusual to place the knight on g7, but it does a fine job – keeping the white king at bay, protecting e6 (after ...f7-f6) and getting ready for a future ...♘f5.

52.♗b1 f6 53.♗a2 ♔d6 54.♔f3 h5

An interesting decision. This pawn is vulnerable to attack by the bishop, but it also fixes the weakness on h4.

55.♔g3 ♔c5 56.♗b3 ♔d4 57.♔f3 ♔d3

58.♗a4 The decisive error, allowing Black to collect a second pawn.

It seems that the endgame after 58.♗a2 ♘f5 59.♔f2 (59.♗xe6? ♘d4+) 59...♔e4 60.♗xe6 ♔xf4 is drawn, even after Black picks up the pawn on h4, though I wouldn't enjoy the task of trying to demonstrate that!

58...♘f5 59.♗b5+ ♔d4 60.♗e8 ♘xh4+ 61.♔g3 ♘f5+ 62.♔f3 ♘g7 63.♗f7 ♔d5 64.♔g6 f5

65.♗f7 ♔d6 66.♔g3 ♔e7 67.♗g6 ♔f6 68.♗h7 ♘e8 White resigned.

But cast an eye back more than a decade, to a time when Carlsen pulled off a similar stunt and won the following position after 100 moves.

Ponomariov-Carlsen
Nice Amber Rapid 2010
position after 39.♖xa5

It was rather impressive that Wesley managed to make anything of this one. It must be said that Nepomniachtchi was playing under duress, being heavily distracted by a scourge of mosquitoes during the game. As his position deteriorated, he could be seen desperately swatting at them.

The next day, Nepomniachtchi tweeted a photograph of his plug-in insect repellent. He made a fierce effort to pull it back the next day, but So steered his way through a game of fascinating complexity.

Ian Nepomniachtchi
Wesley So
CCT FTX Crypto Cup 2021 (sf 2.1)
English Opening, Four Knights Variation

1.c4 ♘f6 2.♘c3 e5 3.♘f3 ♘c6 4.e3 ♗b4 5.♘d5 e4 6.♘g1 0-0 7.♘h3 ♖e8 8.♘hf4 b6 9.♘xb4 ♘xb4 10.b3 d5 11.♗b2 dxc4 12.♗xc4 ♗a6 13.♗xa6 ♘xa6 14.0-0 ♕e7 15.f3 ♖ad8 16.fxe4 ♘xe4 17.d3 ♘b4 18.♖f3 f6 19.♕e2 ♘g5 20.♖g3 ♘e6 21.♘h5 ♔h8 22.♖f1 ♖f8 23.d4 c5 24.a3 ♘d5 25.e4 ♘xd4

NEW FRITZTRAINER DVDs

Let our experts introduce you into the world of Vasily Smyslov! Complete your repertoire with a sound and ambitious setup against the English Opening. Or let Mihail Marin show you how to fight the Semi-Slav, the Chebanenko Slav and the Triangle Setup with the Catalan!

MASTERCLASS VOL. 14: VASILY SMYSLOV *

Vasily Smyslov defeated Mikhail Botvinnik at the second attempt in 1957 and thus became the 7th world champion in chess history, but had to relinquish the title in a rematch the following year. After that Smyslov belonged to the absolute world elite for many years. His performance in the 1982-1985 World Championship cycle was sensational, when he defeated Robert Hübner and Zoltan Ribli one after the other in the candidate matches and only lost in the final to the young Garry Kasparov - Smyslov himself was 62 years old at that time! Smyslov had a particularly deep understanding of chess. Perhaps influenced by music (he was a trained opera singer), his play was characterised by naturalness and harmony. He cultivated a clear positional style and even in sharp tactical positions often relied more on his intuition than on concrete calculation of variations, although he knew how to combine brilliantly when necessary. On the other hand, he shied away from unclear intricacies. Smyslov had a special preference for the (early) exchange of queens as a precursor to his brilliant technique, especially in the endgame, where he was considered an absolute luminary. The 14th World Champion Vladimir Kramnik called Smyslov "the truth in chess". Let our team of experts Yannick Pelletier, Mihail Marin, Karsten Müller and Oliver Reeh introduce you into the world of Vasily Smyslov!

29,90 €

NICHOLAS PERT: A COMPLETE BLACK REPERTOIRE VERSUS THE ENGLISH: 1...e5 *

The English is becoming increasingly popular as White players avoid the heavy theory of 1.e4 or 1.d4 and hope to achieve a small advantage in a safe position. A lot of club players tend to focus on openings against 1.e4 and 1.d4 but neglect to study a response to the English. 1...e5 is a theoretically sound response with good chances of equality or better in all variations, and in this video series provides a complete Black repertoire based on this move. Pert: "I have several years of experience playing 1...e5 against the English, and it is used regularly by many of the world's leading grandmasters. Anish Giri is known for his opening preparation and his ideas feature heavily in the chapters. The repertoire is designed for players who want a complete, independent repertoire against 1.c4. 1...e5 is the 2nd most popular response to the English after 1...Nf6, and doesn't allow direct transpositions into 1.d4 openings. In many of the chapters Black equalises, and when the White players become a bit adventurous or don't know how to handle the positions, Black can hope for an advantage. The two positions that feature most heavily are the Four Knights English, 1.c4 e5 2. Nc3 Nf6 3. Nf3 Nc6 and the systems with early g3, 1.c4 e5 2. g3 c6. In both of these positions I have studied the main variations in depth, but also covered some of the minor lines. The same themes have a habit of coming up regularly and I have attempted to present the main ideas of these key positions as well as the theory in order to help the viewer's understanding of this opening."

29,90 €

MIHAIL MARIN: THE CATALAN VS. THE SEMI-SLAV, CHEBANENKO AND TRIANGLE SETUP *

The Semi-Slav, Chebanenko system and the Slav triangle are solid and flexible weapons for Black. The repertoire examined on this DVD meets them all in a provocative way. In order to avoid reaching a somewhat passive Catalan setup, Black has to get out of his comfort zone and accept the pawn sacrifice on c4. White's compensation typically consists of an advance in development and a space advantage in the centre and play frequently acquires a neo-romantic character. There are lines where it is hard to prove an objective advantage for White in analysis mode, but Black's route to a safe position is not simple, either. In over-the-board play White has excellent chances for maintaining the initiative for a long time. A compact and promising repertoire for active players!

29,90 €

*Expected to be available in July/August

ChessBase GmbH · News: en.chessbase.com · CB Shop: shop.chessbase.com
CHESSBASE DEALER: NEW IN CHESS · P.O. Box 1093 · NL-1810 KB Alkmaar
phone (+31)72 5127137 · fax (+31)72 5158234 · **WWW.NEWINCHESS.COM**

26.♗xd4

It feels like a reflex to capture the knight on d4, when you see that it can be followed by ♖xg7. Surprisingly though, the strongest move was 26.♕d3! and if the knight retreats from d5, g7 falls anyway: 26... g6 (perhaps Black's best option is 26...♘b4 27.axb4 ♘f5 28.♕e2 ♘xg3 29.hxg3 cxb4, with a messy position where White retains some kingside pressure) 27.exd5 gxh5 28.♗xd4 cxd4 29.♕xd4 and Black is struggling.

26...cxd4 27.♖xg7 d3! 28.♕f2 ♕xe4

The queen seems to be trapped in mid-board after White's next move but the pawn on d3 proves to be a crucial defensive resource.

29.♖e1 ♘e3! 30.♖xe3 ♕xe3 31.♕xe3 d2 32.♖xh7+ ♔xh7 33.♘xf6+ ♔g6

33...♖xf6? 34.♕e7+ ♔g6 35.♕xd8 wins

34.♕g3+ ♔f7

So attempts to use the knight as a shield from checks, but in fact it only delays the inevitable perpetual.

35.♕c7+ ♔g6 36.♕g3+ ♔f7 37.♕c7+ ♔e6

38.♕c4+! The final accurate move. 38.♕c6+? loses: 38...♖d6 39.♕e4+ ♔xf6 40.♕f4+ ♔e7 and Black's king can hide behind the ♖d6.

38...♔f5 39.♕e4+ ♔xf6 40.♕f4+ ♔e7 41.♕e3+

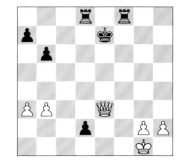

This is the basic problem – Black's king cannot hide on the queenside without letting the d-pawn drop.

41...♔f6 42.♕f4+ ♔e6 43.♕e3+ ♔f5 44.♕f3+ ♔g6 45.♕g4+ ♔f7 46.♕f4+ ♔e7 47.♕e3+ ♔f7 48.♕f4+ ♔e7 Draw.

So won the third game of the match to book his slot in the Final. He enjoyed a little good fortune, as mentioned earlier, but still it was a remarkable achievement to get that far without losing a game.

Patient and pragmatic

Teimour Radjabov has been another consistent performer in the Meltwater Champions Chess Tour. He is patient, pragmatic, and extremely hard to beat, and following the FTX Crypto Cup he sits in third place behind Carlsen and So in the overall standings. He had more than one promising position against Giri in their quarter final match, but a single win in the first set was enough to carry him through.

Radjabov fell behind in his semifinal match with Carlsen, when an uncharacteristic move-order mishap left him with a lifeless position. But Radjabov followed that up by winning a powerful game, showcasing an ambitious idea against Carlsen's Ragozin. With the first set tied 2-2,

the World Champion was visibly rattled, and his post-game interview was comically terse: 'I blundered and he played well. Thank you and see you tomorrow!' was all he could muster.

Teimour Radjabov
Magnus Carlsen
CCT FTX Crypto Cup 2021 (sf 1.4)
Queen's Gambit Declined, Ragozin Variation

1.d4 ♘f6 2.c4 e6 3.♘f3 d5 4.♘c3 ♗b4 5.♗g5 h6 6.♗xf6 ♕xf6 7.♕a4+ ♘c6 8.e3 0-0 9.♖c1 ♕g6

An annoying move. The pressure on the g2-pawn rules out the most natural development with ♗f1-e2.

10.h4

Not strictly a novelty, but 10.♕c2 has been the main theoretical battleground. In his post-game press conference, Radjabov explained that he had prepared 10.h4 for 'someone at the very top level', but got his chance to use it against Magnus.

10...♖d8 11.h5 ♕f6 12.♖h4

This unusual development of the rook supports the centre, and introduces the idea of ♖h4-f4. Carlsen goes for a break in the centre.

12...e5

What could be more natural than a central break, in response to White's eccentric setup? This move turns out to be a serious error, but one of the computer's preferred moves, 12...♕f5, looks extremely awkward to me.
13.cxd5 ♖xd5 14.dxe5 ♗xc3+ 15.♖xc3 ♘xe5 16.♕e8+ ♔h7

17.♖f4 This natural move turns out to let Black off the hook.

17.♖d4 was the right way to press White's advantage. Although it feels dubious to invite 17...♘xf3+ 18.gxf3 ♖xd4 19.exd4 White is winning in spite of the crippled structure, with threats of ♗d3+ and ♖c7. 19...♕e6+ 20.♔e3 ♕xe8 21.♖xe8 offers Black no respite.

17...♕d6 Defending the knight and threatening ...♖d1+, but Radjabov's next move consolidates nicely.

17...♕b6! launches a brisk counterattack: 18.b4 (18.♘xe5 ♕xb2 spells disaster)

ANALYSIS DIAGRAM

18...♗g4!! 19.♕xa8 ♗xf3 20.gxf3 ♕xb4!? (20...♘xf3+ amounts to the same thing) 21.♖xb4 ♘xf3+ 22.♔e2 ♘g1+ 23.♔e1 ♘f3+, with a charming repetition pointed out by Chess24.

18.♗e2

18...f5 An ugly move, but unlike the previous variation, there is no follow-up after 18...♗g4 19.♕xa8.
19.♘d4 c6 20.♘xf5 ♕d8 21.♕xd8 ♖xd8 22.♘d4

Radjabov has a clean extra pawn, and wrapped up the technical task without much fuss.
22...♗d7 23.♖e4 ♖e8 24.♖c5 ♘f7 25.♗d3 ♔h8 26.♖xe8+ ♖xe8 27.b4 ♘d6 28.♗g6 ♖e7 29.a4 ♔g8 30.♔e2 ♘e4 31.♖c2 ♘f6 32.b5 cxb5 33.axb5 a6 34.bxa6 bxa6 35.♖b2 ♗e8 36.♖b8 ♔f8 37.♘f5 ♖e6 38.♖a8 ♘d5 39.♗xe8 ♖xe8 40.♖xa6 ♘f4+ 41.♔f3 ♘xh5 42.g4 ♘f6 43.♘xh6 ♘e4 44.♘f5 ♘g5+ 45.♔g2 ♖b8 46.♘d4 ♔f7 47.♖a5 ♘e4 48.♖e5 ♘f6 49.f3 g6 50.♔g3 ♖b1 51.♖b5 ♖xb5 52.♘xb5 g5 53.♘c3 ♔g6 54.f4
Black resigned.

Radjabov got knocked out the next day, leaving him in the 3rd-4th playoff against Nepomniachtchi, while Carlsen and So met in the Final for the third time this season.

Shocking?

If the 'problem' of short draws had simmered during the prelims, it boiled over on the first day of the 3rd-4th playoff match. All four games were drawn by repetition, in record time. I think it's fair to say that the predominant reaction went like this: 'It's an insult to fans, and an insult to Caissa herself. How dare they!' A few shrugged their shoulders. 'The players are disappointed and exhausted, and nobody much cares for the 3rd/4th playoff match anyway. Be patient – there will be blood tomorrow.'

I would add that, although four consecutive draws looks like a conspiracy of indolence, it was just as plausibly explained by an accidental avalanche of pacifism. Radjabov plays White in the first game. Surely tired and disappointed, and with no fresh powder against the Grünfeld, he is satisfied with a draw. Nepomniachtchi, with White in the second, has no special desire to bash his head against the Berlin, so a draw merely restores the balance. With two games to go Radjabov can safely burn a second White, knowing that he only has to survive one game with Black if Nepomniachtchi avoids a repetition in the fourth. As it is, Nepomniachtchi punts an Italian instead, but after a few seconds' reflection decides that 2-2 is a perfectly satisfactory result for the day. In other words, one doesn't set out to make draws in all the White games. But when the players alternate their Whites, both lacking energy and fresh opening ideas, four repetitions is not such a shocking outcome.

However you slice it, it remains a rotten outcome for the spectators. Radjabov's provocative tweet did little to endear him to his critics: 'Finally, as today was a short day, I had time to read comments of amateur chess

A novelty. During the live broadcast the rate of the bitcoin was followed. On the first day of the Final the $100,000 of the prize-money to be paid in bitcoin had dropped considerably. By the end of the FTX Crypto Cup it had recovered to $ 85,000.

players about our matches.' In this case, perhaps it were more circumspect to apply that old-fashioned wisdom once associated with the British Royal Family: 'Never complain, never explain'.

The Final

It's a rare sight to see Carlsen making quick draws with the white pieces, but on that first day of the Final, while Radjabov and Nepomniachtchi laid down their weapons, Carlsen was also seen making bland draws against Wesley So's Berlin Defence. It must be said that the backdrop was rather different, as Carlsen had got off to an excellent start, winning the first game with Black. As a result, a draw with White in the second was a rational choice to edge toward closing out the set. When Wesley So pulled back to 1½-1½ in the third game, one might have expected Carlsen to use his White in the fourth game. No such luck – we got a repeat of the arid 5.♖e1 Berlin from Game 2. You can count on Magnus for a frank explanation: 'I felt like shit', he explained afterwards, and in the circumstances he was satisfied with the 2-2 scoreline.

The second day brought considerably more action. The match between Nepomniachtchi and Radjabov exploded into life, with Nepomniachtchi coming out on top. Meanwhile, Carlsen got off to a flying start with this beautiful endgame squeeze.

NOTES BY
Peter Heine Nielsen

Magnus Carlsen
Wesley So
CCT FTX Crypto Cup 2021 (final 2.1)
Queen's Gambit Declined, Semi-Tarrasch

1.d4 ♘f6 2.c4 e6 3.♘f3 d5 4.♘c3 c5

5.e3!? Here, 5.cxd5 is the main move. Magnus used it to beat Giri in an excellent attacking game last

However you slice it, it remains a rotten outcome for the spectators

year. But recently So has been efficient after 5...cxd4!?, steering the game towards a drawish ending. And so, Magnus changes the course of events by... steering towards another drawish ending!

5...dxc4 6.♗xc4 a6 7.0-0 b5 8.♗e2 ♗b7 9.dxc5

This is what Karjakin played by transposition against Magnus in the 2016 World Championship match in New York. This move was introduced by Vladimir Kramnik, who showed that

Black's endgame job is far from easy. In 2016, Magnus played 9...♘c6!?, drawing effortlessly, but improvements for White have been found since then. Ironically enough, it was Kramnik who, in a later game, introduced the way for Black to play, thus effectively neutralizing his own idea!

9...♗xc5 10.♕xd8+ ♔xd8 11.♘d2 ♔e7 12.♘b3 ♘bd7!

This is Kramnik's idea. Black happily gives up the bishop pair, hoping that his central control and more active

king will secure the balance. Here, in an earlier online game vs. Wesley So, Magnus tried 13.♘a5 ♖ab8 14.♘xb7 ♖xb7 15.♗d2, but now he tries a different twist:

13.♖d1!? Not threatening ♖xd7+, since ...♘xd7 would still cover the c5-bishop, but more of a useful waiting move before declaring intentions. Black obviously has many decent moves, and Wesley chooses the most obvious one, not giving White a second chance to grab the bishop pair.

13...♗b6 14.a4 b4 15.a5!

As Bent Larsen stated: opposite-coloured bishop endings are perhaps often drawn, but when they are *very* winning

The point. White uses the vulnerability of the bishop to create instability in Black's queenside pawn chain.
15...♗a7 16.♘a4 ♗d5 17.♘d4 ♖hb8 18.♗d2! ♘c5 19.♘xc5 ♗xc5

20.♖ac1! Just like on move 18, White is not afraid of the pawn isolation, even though Black has it beautifully blockaded with full control of the d5-square.
20...♗xd4 21.exd4

It may look as if Black is perfectly fine, and it's true that if you put the b-pawn back to b5, he would indeed be better. But this detail is very important. Here, the weakness of the black queenside pawns makes the difference. Black cannot play 21...♖c8, since this would lose the b4-pawn, and as he also has to defend the a6-pawn, Black has no reasonable way to activate his pieces. In short: details matter!
21...♔d7 22.♗f4 ♖b7 23.h4!

Quite an extraordinary move, but a good one! With Black lacking active options, White's job is to improve his own position, and this move very much does so. Apart from trivialities like avoiding bottom-rank mates, more relevantly it leaves Black with a structural dilemma. 23...h5 would weaken his kingside structure, but allowing White to go h5 means that h6 also becomes a possibility, and after ...h6 the g7-pawn will be fixed as a weakness. Wesley So is trying to create some kind of active counterplay, but that just makes things worse.

23...♗b3 24.♖d3 ♗a4 25.♗e5 ♗b5? The immediate 25...♘d5 was a better fighting chance.

26.♗f3! Technically, this solves the problem of the a6-pawn, but the price was losing control of the long diagonal. If 26...♗xd3 27.♗xb7, White enters the seventh rank via c7, so Black's reply is forced.
26...♘d5

27.♗xd5! An impressive decision. But, as Bent Larsen stated: opposite-coloured bishops endings are perhaps often drawn, but when they are winning, they are *very* winning. Black simply has zero counterplay in the following.
27...exd5 28.♖g3 g6 29.♖c5 ♗c6 30.♖f3 f5 31.h5

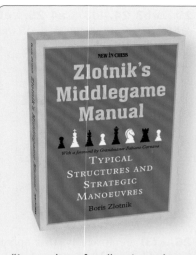
A quick impression may suggest that Black's position looks like a fortress, but White enters via the h-file, and there is absolutely no defence against that plan.

31...♖b5 32.♖c1 ♖e8 33.hxg6 hxg6 34.♖h3

Threatening ♖h7+, winning a piece. So Black has to defend the c6-bishop.

34...♖e6 35.♖h7+ ♔d8 36.b3 g5 37.♗c7+!? ♔e8 38.♗b6

Now the rook on b5 is completely shut out of the game!

38...f4 39.♖g7

And with no reasonable moves to play, So resigned. At best, he'll now lose his kingside pawns, but in addition, his rook is trapped at b5, and moving his bishop allows ♖1c7, so resignation is fully in order.

An impressive and instructive strategical gem by Magnus.

■ ■ ■

Wesley struck back immediately, and two more draws (including, dare I mention, one more ♕e4+/♕d4 Berlin) landed the players in the blitz tiebreak, where this article began by describing Carlsen's back-rank mate pratfall from the first blitz game. Curiously, that game featured another Orangutan Opening again, which had failed to deliver on its inspirational promise. Carlsen fell back on another tried-and-true technique – a change of clothes. His new blue T-shirt brought him a must-win with Black, and another in the Armageddon game that followed.

So followed suit. When Carlsen equalised the score in the blitz,

Wesley tried a new T-shirt for the Armageddon, but to no avail.

Magnus Carlsen
Wesley So
CCT FTX Crypto Cup 2021 (final 3.3)
Italian Game, Giuoco Piano

1.e4 e5 2.♘f3 ♘c6 3.♗c4 ♘f6 4.d3 ♗c5 5.0-0 h6 6.c3 0-0 7.b4 ♗b6 8.a4 a6 9.♘bd2 d6 10.♖e1 ♘e7 11.d4 exd4 12.cxd4 d5 13.e5! ♘h5

White's kingside majority is a major strategic asset, but Black strives for active piece play (...♘e7-g6, ...♘h5-f4, ...f7-f6, ...♗c8-g4, combined with pressure against d4). However, So was already looking dissatisfied, correctly sensing that his counterplay would arrive too slowly.

14.♗f1 ♘f4 15.♘b3 ♘eg6 16.a5 ♗a7

17.♗xf4

I really like this unpretentious move and the follow-up 18.♕d2. Why give up a bishop for a knight? Doing it before ...f7-f6 means that the f4-knight can't be supported by opening the f-file. It also rules out an arrangement such as ♗g4/♘e6.

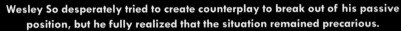

Wesley So desperately tried to create counterplay to break out of his passive position, but he fully realized that the situation remained precarious.

Connecting the rooks (with 18.♕d2) is an afterthought, but it feels nice.

17...♘xf4 18.♕d2 ♘g6 19.♘c5 f6 20.♗d3

20...f5

Not the move Black wanted to play, but 20...♘e7 21.exf6 ♖xf6 22.♘e5 looked even worse.

21.♗c2 ♖e8 22.g3 ♗xc5 23.bxc5

Strategically, Black is busted, but in a blitz game there are no certainties at this stage, especially since a draw is all So requires.

23...♗e6 24.♖ab1 ♖b8 25.♖e3 ♘e7 26.♖eb3 ♕c8 27.♘h4 ♖f8 28.♘g2 ♗d7 29.h4 ♗a4 30.♖3b2

30...♗xc2 30...♗b5 31.♗d3 c6 would succeed in blocking the b-file, but after 32.♗c2! White's rooks can look for new employment on the kingside, while the black bishop is locked out forever.

Wesley So tried a new T-shirt for the Armageddon, but to no avail

31.♕xc2 ♘c6 32.♕c3

32...g5 Risky, of course, but So obviously felt this was essential before the screws tightened with ♘f4 and h4-h5. In fact, 32...f4 33.♘xf4 ♕g4 would have created real practical problems, due to the threat of ...♖xf4, along with pressure against d4 and a5.

33.hxg5 hxg5 34.f4!

34...♔g7 34...g4 35.♘e3 ♘e7 36.c6! ♘xc6 37.♘xd5 is comfortably winning for White.

35.♔f2 ♖h8 36.fxg5 ♖h2 37.♕f3 ♘xd4 38.♕xd5 ♘c6 39.e6 ♕d8 40.♕d7+ ♕xd7 41.exd7 ♖d8 42.♖d2 ♘e5 43.♖xb7 ♔g6 44.♖xc7

Black resigned. ∎

The Marvel of Morphy

Paul Morphy's eternal legacy and the greatest Morphiana collection in the world

Paul Morphy photographed by Mathew Brady, one of the earliest photographers in America. Brady was celebrated for his portraits of politicians and his photographs of the American Civil War.

He dazzled his contem-poraries with his genius and virtuosity, and became an instant legend in the few years that his chess career lasted. Paul Morphy (1837-1884) remains one of the greatest champions of all time, and everything connected with him exerts an inescapable lure. **DIRK JAN TEN GEUZENDAM** revisits the high points in the American's life as he talks to David DeLucia about his wonderful Morphy collection — which happens to be on the market (as is the rest of his collection).

David DeLucia's chess library is an endless treasure vault. Described in this magazine in 2010 as 'the finest chess collection in the world', it's so vast and all-encompassing that it could easily be separated in a number of collections that would be splendid in their own right. The landmarks of chess publishing are all there, from the very first books – the Lucena of 1497 and the first edition of Damiano of 1512 – to fine copies of any classic you can think of. Books signed by the

'In 1857, when Morphy won the First American Congress, he was twenty years old and a few years later he was virtually done with the game'

authors, manuscripts, iconic clocks, photographs, scoresheets, letters – no matter what you want to see, you'll probably find it there.

Amid this general interest, DeLucia has always had a fascination for the World Champions and their closest rivals. His Capablanca and Alekhine collections are impressive and wide-ranging, but his Fischer and Lasker collections are truly phenomenal in size and depth.

Still, it's the much smaller Paul Morphy collection that is closest to his heart. 'It's not the most valuable, but it probably gives me the greatest joy,' says David DeLucia as we talk via Skype. 'I would probably rank it number one of the subsets. Morphy was a great player. He really was one of those players that changed the way the game is looked at. I love going over his games. And the sad part about it, he only played for like two years. In 1857, when he won the First American Congress, he was twenty years old and a few years later he was virtually done with the game.'

The reason we speak about his Morphy collection is not only our shared fascination with the most remarkable player of the 19th century. Recently, DeLucia acquired a number of Morphy items from the estate of the late Dale Brandreth, the collector, publisher and bookseller who held

Morphy in equally high regard. With these items DeLucia more or less completed his Morphy collection. There is still Morphiana out there, but it is uncertain if they will ever resurface and what they would add to his collection. A few months ago, a small thank-you note signed by Morphy was sold at an auction in Sweden for 3,000 euros. DeLucia let it go because to his mind the note had 'no content'.

Complete sight of the board
The greatness of Paul Morphy has always been undisputed. His understanding of the game far exceeded that of his contemporaries, and the brilliance and rapidity of his play made him more famous than any chess player before him. These days, his star status seems to have waned somewhat. The weakness of his opponents is often mentioned, and any amateur so inclined can dissect Morphy's games with an engine and

A signed 'carte de visite' of Paul Morphy. These were small photographs the size of a visiting card that were popular in the 1860s, traded between friends and collected.

Another Mathew Brady photo. Louis Paulsen and Paul Morphy are sitting at the chessboard surrounded by the participants and officials of the First American Congress in 1857.

look for errors. All this feels irrelevant when speaking about a player who was at his peak 160 years ago. Perhaps we should listen to 21-year-old Bobby Fischer, who fastidiously played over several hundreds of Morphy's games without a computer. In 1964, when he drew up his famous list of 10 best players of all time, Fischer concluded: 'Morphy was perhaps the most accurate player who ever lived. He had complete sight of the board and never blundered, in spite of the fact that he played quite rapidly, rarely taking more than five minutes to decide a move. (...) I am continually surprised and entertained by his ingenuity.'

As said, Morphy's chess playing career was remarkably short. The 1857 American Chess Congress in New York – the first American championship, you could say – was not only the first but also the only tournament Morphy ever played in. Before the Congress he mainly played off-hand games in private, often at odds, and a couple of brief matches against American players. After he had won the Congress, his fans challenged any strong European player to come over and play a match for good stakes. When no reaction came, Morphy decided to go over to Europe himself.

Bobby Fischer concluded: 'Morphy was perhaps the most accurate player who ever lived'

He had time on his hands, after all, as he had finished his legal studies, but was still too young to practise law. The matches he won in great style in Europe, including a convincing win against Adolf Anderssen – the winner of the first great international tournament in London in 1851 – cemented his international fame. They must also, however, have left him with the feeling that there was nothing more to be achieved and, more importantly, that there were more useful

things in life to do. He wanted to work as a lawyer and certainly didn't want to be regarded as a professional chess player.

Five favourites
In spite of the shortness of Morphy's career, DeLucia's collection is replete with manuscripts and memorabilia from all stages of Morphy's life when chess was his passion. When I ask him to list his five favourite Morphy items, he thinks briefly and then enumerates five items that feel like giving a bird's-eye view of one of the most unforgettable chess careers of all time.

'First and foremost' he names the inlaid mother-of-pearl chessboard that Morphy got on his twelfth birthday. On that day, Morphy played a blindfold game against his uncle Ernest, and as he made his twentieth move he commented 'I must win now', whereupon Dr. A.P. Ford, a chess friend of his uncle's, who was visiting, took him to the adjoining room and presented him with the chessboard.

Morphy was clearly a prodigious talent, and as the well-known story goes, he learnt the game as a kid by watching his father and his uncle Ernest play. And also that one night, when Ernest was waiting for his father, young Paul suggested they play a game, and proved that he could hold his own against his uncle. This story was debunked by Frederic Milnes Edge, who accompanied Morphy on his trip to Europe and wrote the colourful *The Exploits and Triumphs in Europe of Paul Morphy*: 'I sorrowfully confess that my hero's unromantic regard for the truth makes him characterize the above statement as humbug and an impossibility.'

As his second favourite item, DeLucia chooses the game scores, all signed, of the first three games Morphy played against James Thompson in the First American Chess Congress.

The inlaid mother-of-pearl chessboard that Morphy got as a present on his twelfth birthday.

Paul Morphy

1837 Born 22 June in New Orleans, Louisiana

1850 As a 12-year-old he beats Hungarian master Löwenthal 3-0

1857 Wins First American Congress in New York, defeats Louis Paulsen in final: 6-2

1858-59 Trip to Europe; is brilliant in countless offhand games, defeating all opponents, many in games at odds or blindfold. Stuns everyone with blindfold simuls against up to eight players.

1858 Defeats chess professional Daniel Harwitz in a match: 5½-2½

1858 Defeats Adolf Anderssen, the winner of the 1851 London tournament, in a match: 8-3

1859 Returns from Europe to a hero's welcome in a tour of the major American cities

1859 Abandons competitive chess

1884 Having suffered from mental illness in his later years, he suffers a stroke and dies on 10 July at the age of 47

And number three is a photo of Morphy taken by Mathew Brady, who became famous himself with his Civil War photos. From a modern perspective there seem to be fairly few Morphy photos, but given that photography was still in its infancy, the number of photos in the collection clearly show what a celebrity he was. Besides a few Mathew Brady photos, there are cabinet photos, stereo views and even tiny ferrographs with Morphy's countenance.

The fourth favourite that DeLucia mentions is a 27-page handwritten draft of the speech that Morphy gave on his glorious return from Europe at the 'presentation of testimonials' in New York. From the moment he left the British passenger liner *Persia*, which had taken him across the Atlantic, Morphy was dragged to dinners and receptions, with the welcome festivities culminating in a massively attended evening at University Hall. In 1972, Bobby

Fischer may have been received by Mayor Lindsay of New York and given the city's gold medal in front of a thousand people after his win against Spassky in Reykjavik, but that reception pales in comparison with the welcome Morphy got. There were endless tributes and he was lavished with presents, the most stunning being a gold and silver chess set adorned with precious stones.

Morphy thanked everyone in his speech and spoke words that eerily heralded the distance he would soon be keeping from his favourite game and give a first taste of his disenchantment with competitive chess: 'Chess never has been and never can be aught more than a recreation. It should not be indulged in to the detriment of other and more serious avocations – should not absorb the mind or engross the thoughts of

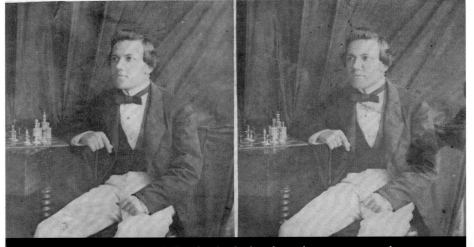

A stereoview of Paul Morphy. Looked at through a stereoscope these almost identical photographs created an illusion of depth.

PAUL MORPHY

S. S. Nichols, Reporter.   Commenced at 1.40 P.M.
                            October 6. 1857.

National Chess Congress.

Section *First*,   Game *First*.

Between *Paul Morphy* and *James Thompson*.

Game score, signed by Morphy, of the first game he played in the 1857 American Congress against James Thompson.

those who worship at its shrine; but should be kept in the background and restrained within its proper province. As a mere game, a relaxation from the severer pursuits of life, it is deserving of high commendation. It is not only the most delightful and scientific, but the most moral of amusements. Unlike other games in which lucre is the end and aim of the contestants, it recommends itself to the wise by the fact that its mimic battles are fought for no prize but honour. It is eminently and emphatically the philosopher's game.'

Morphy's ideas about chess did not become any rosier after he had stopped playing matches and essen-

tially given up chess. The fifth favourite item that David DeLucia chooses is a letter to his friend Daniel Fiske, the organizer of the 1857 Congress and the editor of *The Chess Monthly* of which Morphy was a contributor. The letter was written on February 4, 1863, in Paris, where Morphy had gone together with his mother and sister, having temporarily left New Orleans because of the Civil War. Fiske had forwarded an invitation from the Vienna Chess Club to him, but against the background of the war, Morphy could only see the futility of chess. 'We are all following with intense anxiety the fortunes of the tremendous conflict now raging beyond the Atlantic, for upon this issue depends our all in life. Under such circumstances you will readily understand that I should feel little disposed to engage in the objectless strife of the chess board. Besides you will remember that as far back as two years ago, I stated to you in New York my firm determination to abandon chess altogether. I am more strongly confirmed than ever in the belief that the time devoted to chess is literally frittered away. It is, to be sure, a most exhilarating sport, but it is only a sport; and it is not to be wondered at that such as have been passionately addicted to the charming pastime, should one day

ask themselves whether sober reason does not advise its utter dereliction. I have, for my own part, resolved not to be moved from my purpose of not engaging in chess hereafter.'

Preternaturally small

Morphy kept his word and did not compete seriously anymore. Sadly, he entered a stage in his life in which, instead of 'the pride of chess', he became 'the sorrow of chess'. His later years were troubled and he died young, from a stroke, at the age of 47. After his death his family were not very keen on him being permanently associated with chess either. As a result, chess books in which he wrote his name are rare, because his relatives cut out his name whenever they could.

Despite his family's efforts Morphy the chess player remained a celebrity, even if his fame was probably never greater than during his lifetime. Two conspicuous items in the collection are reminiscent of his years of triumph. Both the bust and the hand made by Eugène-Louis Lequesne are testimony to the sensation and delight Paul Morphy created with his chess. Lequesne was the leading French sculptor of the day. He was also a strong chess player and one of Morphy's opponents in the blindfold exhibition against eight opponents in

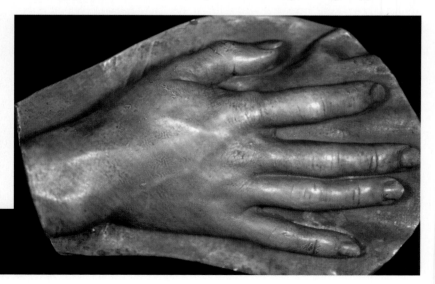

The life cast of Morphy's hand by Eugène-Louis Lequesne: 16 centimetres long, 11 wide and 3 centimetres thick.

68 NEW IN CHESS

Lequesne's Morphy bust amid other collectibles in David DeLucia's chess library.

Paris in September 1858 (and one of the two players to manage a draw) – an exhibition that lasted close to 10 hours, during which Morphy was said not to have eaten or drunk anything.

Lequesne was so enraptured by Morphy's genius that he asked him to sit for him so he could sculpt his bust. While he was at it, he also took a life cast of his hand. I ask David DeLucia to measure the hand and he tells me it is 16 centimetres long, 11 centimetres wide and 3 centimetres thick. That's a very small hand, and the measurements confirm its description by G.A. MacDonnell in his book *Chess Life-Pictures* (1883). MacDonnell was an experienced player and writer who met Morphy during his stay in London in 1858. Thinking back to that moment, he wrote: 'Morphy was short of stature, but well and even gracefully proportioned, save that his hands and feet were preternaturally small, the former being very white and well-shaped.'

Morphy's delicate features and modest height have often been described. In the book of the First American Congress, Fiske wrote: 'Physically, Paul Morphy is of short stature and slight build. He has the dark eye and hair of the South, and

betrays in many ways his Gallic descent. His eye is soft and expressive and assumes an expression of brilliancy whenever he is examining an interesting position. His memory is wonderfully good, and his comprehension quick and active.'

As is the case with all the greatest players of our time, exceptional

Morphy could just as easily recall months-old games or information from chess books as reproduce melodies and musical airs he had heard at the opera

memory was one of Morphy's strengths. He could just as easily recall months-old games or information from chess books as reproduce melodies and musical airs he had heard at the opera. About his blindfold exhibition against eight oppo-

nents, Edge writes: 'Next morning, Morphy actually awakened me at seven o'clock, and told me that if I would get up, he would dictate to me the moves of yesterday's games. I never saw him in better spirits, or less fatigued, than on that occasion, as he showed me, for two long hours, the hundreds of variations depending on the play of the previous day, with such rapidity that I found it hard to follow the thread of his combinations.'

Morphy vs Paulsen

Morphy's modest height also clearly shows in a lithograph based on a photograph of Louis Paulsen and Morphy taken at the 1857 Congress. While Paulsen, who admired Morphy and had no doubt that he was the better player, tries to pose as modestly as possible, he still towers over his opponent.

Looking at the confrontation between Paulsen and Morphy in New York, you also realize what a far cry from modern practice that contest was. Paulsen and Morphy met in the final match of the 16-player knockout contest, which only seems logical, since they were the clear favourites. However, it was actually pure chance, because lots were drawn for every round, and the two might easily have been paired against one another at any stage.

Equally remarkable is what happened three weeks before the final, during the first round. That first round consisted of 8 matches from which the players who first scored three wins proceeded to the next round. While the round was still in progress, Paulsen played Morphy... in a blindfold simul! Having already won his first-round match, Paulsen, who was famous for his blindfold play, had said that he was ready to take on four opponents blindfold. And he also invited Morphy! Morphy accepted, provided he was allowed to play blindfolded as well. The outcome must have been embarrassing for the German from Iowa.

Louis Paulsen
Paul Morphy
New York blindfold simul 1857

position after 23.♕xc7

White is two pawns up, but Black's attack is overwhelming. Morphy called out his next move and announced mate in five.
23...♖xg2+ 24.♔xg2 ♕h3+ 25.♔f2 ♕h2+ 26.♔f3 ♖f8+ 27.♕f7 ♖xf7 Mate.

Looking at the lithograph with Paulsen, and seeing the two of them sitting there, it is tempting to think that being Paul Morphy cannot always have been easy. While the genius from New Orleans was known for his quick and unwavering play, Paulsen had the reputation of being an extremely slow player. There was officially no time-limit on the moves, which required extreme patience from Morphy, as can be seen from the sheets in DeLucia's collection, on which assistants wrote down the minutes the players spent on their moves. Particularly tedious was the second game. The total amount of time that Morphy spent on moves that took him more than five minutes was a modest 25 minutes. In Paulsen's case it was 11 hours! Small wonder that Morphy lost that game when he started a sequence of moves with the second move, probably because he was exhausted or bored to death at that point.

That loss affected him and he also lost the next game, but he won the match 6-2 (+5, -1, =2). The most famous moment of the final match came in Game 6:

The hare and the tortoise. While moves came easily and naturally to Paul Morphy, Louis Paulsen tended to think for many hours during a game.

Louis Paulsen
Paul Morphy
New York First American Congress 1857 (6)

position after 17.♕a6

Here, after thinking for 12 minutes, Morphy played:
17...♕xf3! Typically, Paulsen thought for an hour(!) before taking the queen, and Black won in 28 moves. Steinitz was so impressed by the position after 17...♕xf3 that he put a diagram of the position printed in gold on the cover of his book *Modern Chess Instructor* (1889). The remaining moves were: **18.gxf3 ♖g6+ 19.♔h1 ♗h3 20.♖d1 ♗g2+ 21.♔g1 ♗xf3+ 22.♔f1 ♗g2+ 23.♔g1 ♗h3+ 24.♔h1 ♗xf2 25.♕f1 ♗xf1 26.♖xf1 ♖e2 27.♖a1 ♖h6 28.d4 ♗e3** 0-1.

The history of the collection
Every great collection has a history that is worth telling. A history that not only documents the provenance of the collection, but also reveals what a special and motley breed collectors are. David DeLucia's Morphy collection could never have existed without the efforts of the first great Morphy collector, David Lawson, the author of Morphy's biography *Paul Morphy, The Pride and Sorrow of Chess.* Born in Glasgow, Scotland, in 1886, Lawson moved to America at a young

The total amount of time that Morphy spent on moves that took him more than five minutes was a modest 25 minutes. In Paulsen's case it was 11 hours!

age and lived in Morphy's native city of New Orleans for a couple of years before moving to New York, where he worked as an engineer. Lawson was a tireless collector, who not only chased Morphiana in the United States, but also traced Morphy's footsteps during his European tour.

His book was published in 1976, when Lawson was 90 years old. Shortly after its publication he sold his collection to Dale Brandreth, the chess publisher, book dealer and collector from Hockessin, Delaware. Brandreth collected and traded on a grand scale, and had a second home just for his many thousands of books. But more about that later.

Lawson might have decided that the time had come to part with his Morphy collection, but apparently he was not entirely ready yet. DeLucia vividly remembers what Brandreth had told him about the biggest acquisition in his career.

'Dale had gone down to visit him, they agreed on the price, then Dale went back to Delaware and came back with another guy to help him. They go there and they start packing up the stuff. And Dale just gets the feeling that it's not all the stuff that he remembers seeing when he was the first time there. So he pulls his helper aside and he tells him, you talk to David Lawson, you keep him busy, I think there's some stuff missing. So the guy starts talking to Lawson, while Dale is going through the house. He goes into Lawson's bedroom, he stoops down, looks under the bed and there is a box and it's all Morphy stuff. He takes it down and goes back. He looks around, he opens up a closet and there's another box of Morphy stuff. And it seems that what he had seen the first time, he has now. I don't know what he said to Lawson, but whenever Dale would talk about David Lawson, it was not in a good

light, because he felt like he had been cheated.'

Dale Brandreth kept most of what he bought from Lawson, but not all. To recoup some of his investment he sold part of it to four or five collectors. Essentially, what they obtained would become the basis of DeLucia's Morphy collection, as over the years he would buy their (entire) collections.

Fist fights
The first of these items he bought in 1991 from Sam Ennis, a collector of chess Americana, who lived in a trailer in the middle of nowhere in Madison, Wisconsin. 'Sam was always proud to say that 80 per cent of his disposable income was spent on accumulating chess items. He was always short of money and then he got very broke and he wanted to sell the whole collection. He had several signed items, including Morphy's

childhood arithmetic book and Morphy's childhood French book. I don't know how Sam made his money. The only story I remember, which I thought was kind of humorous, was that he told me that he used to love to drink. And when he drank, he'd get into fist fights all the time. And I said to him, just innocently, what made you stop? And he said, when I started losing all the fights!'

Sam Ennis might have sold his collection, but this did not end his love for Morphiana. The next year there was an auction in a small town in Massachusetts of a number of Morphy items, including his walking stick and Lequesne's hand. There was little publicity and DeLucia believed it was going to be a great opportunity. But to his amazement he was outbid on most items by an unknown opponent. 'About a week later, I got a call from Sam Ennis. He was the other bidder. It was just the two of us. He said, you know David, I really wanted to see some of this stuff, but I am really hurting now for money. Can I sell it all back to you for what I paid for it? And I ended up paying him the amount plus the commission and everything. He wanted to keep the items with him for a week. That was fine with me. Sam was an

A cabinet photo (a photograph mounted on a stiff piece of cardboard) of Paul Morphy taken in Paris around 1863 after he had abandoned competitive chess.

honourable guy. And one week later he sent me the stuff.'

Bring your check book

And so, at some point David DeLucia had obtained more or less what David Lawson had owned, with the exception of the part of the Morphy collection that Dale Brandreth had kept for

himself. The big day came in March 2006. 'I would always call Dale, we talked a lot. He loved talking chess and I enjoyed talking to him because he was very knowledgeable. He was a real chess historian. He also knew some of these people. He would tell you that he was playing in Toronto at some time and Bobby Fischer was playing there. Bobby was like 12 years old, and he had just been beaten and sat crying in a corner. He had a lot of these stories. One day, I called Dale and asked, do you have any top-notch items? I am only three hours from your house. I'd love to come down and do some business. And he said, yeah, let me think about it and I'll put something together. Then nothing happened, and all of a sudden he called and said, listen, I have some really nice items here, some nice Morphy items and some other things. And I said, can you tell me what they are? And he said, no, it's better that you come down. And I said, how do I know how much to bring and he said, just bring your check book. And I went down to his "Chess Cathedral", a term coined by his son-in-law, and that's when he had the Morphy chessboard, the signed Mathew Brady photo, a game score from the First American Chess Congress, a Morphy letter, the Morphy analysis of the game Montgomery-Alis that he did for *The Chess Monthly*, and some other things, too.'

The two collectors continued their phone calls for many years, but it was only after Dale Brandreth's death in 2019, when his wife Alice had asked him to come down to Delaware, that David DeLucia acquired his final Morphy items. There was another game annotated in Morphy's hand, two more signed scoresheets from the First American Congress and some of the timesheets of the Paulsen-Morphy final.

And by some miracle he found an album that he had asked Brandreth about, and that Brandreth had searched for in vain: an album that Brandreth had bought at an auction

'There are so many books on the floor, and boxes and what not, I can't even walk to the other side of the room'

where DeLucia's bid via a friend had been insufficient. An album with some Morphy items, including a short letter signed by him. 'I didn't know what to expect when I went down there. At the end, Dale had dementia and Alice had warned me that it was an absolute mess. I get there and I open up the door, and I can't believe it. Not only are there books everywhere on the shelves, there are books on all the furniture, the kitchen table... There's a sofa in the living room full of books, books all over the floor. When I say books, I am not talking about hundreds, I am talking about thousands. Books going up to a meter, maybe to a

meter and a half, on both sides of the hallway, you can hardly get through. All I can keep thinking to myself is, oh my goodness, what a mess. What did I get myself into? There are so many books on the floor, and boxes and what not, I can't even walk to the other side of the room. And for some reason there is a box that is in front of the fireplace, and on top of the box, there is a book that I had never seen. So I walk over some of the books, I almost fall slipping on one of the books, and I get down to the box and I bend down and pick it up. And to my chagrin it's not a chess book, it was just some meaningless book. And as I put it back on the pile, I notice a small red leather album, and I knew right away that it was the album that Dale couldn't find. It still amazes me that in a house that had probably a hundred thousand books in it, when I first walk in, I almost went straight for this Morphy item.'

The future of the collection

As most collectors David DeLucia fully realizes that the joy of collecting remains a tender balance between the excitement of the hunt and the gratification of ownership of something unique and special – and the knowledge that one day your collection will pass into other hands.

In the course of the past few years he has cut the knot and decided that he is ready to sell the harvest of 35 years of collecting. On the Sotheby's website, a film can be viewed called *A Life Less Ordinary, How David DeLucia built a chess collection unlike any other*, inviting potential buyers to contact the auction house.

DeLucia's main wish is for the collection to find a good home where it can be on permanent display in a museum for all to enjoy – if not an institution, then an individual who will continue to add to it. 'I think it's not only important to collect these great players, these geniuses, for their games, but it's also important to paint a picture of who they were outside of

Collecting Paul Morphy

The first and greatest Paul Morphy collector, and a ground-breaking pioneer in Morphy research, was **David Lawson** (1886-1980). All through his life Lawson hunted for Morphiana. In 1976 he published the authoritative biography, *Paul Morphy, The Pride and Sorrow of Chess*, which remains a huge source of information about the most celebrated player of the 19th century.

After the publication of his book, Lawson sold his complete collection to **Dale Brandreth** (1931-2019). Brandreth was not only a collector, but also a chess book dealer and the publisher of Caissa Editions.

Over the past three decades the American collector **David DeLucia** gradually acquired all the items that Brandreth had kept for himself plus most of what he had sold to others. Today DeLucia has the biggest collection of Morphy items in private or public hands in the world.

the royal game. I am confident that the sub-set collections of the champions from Paul Morphy through Bobby Fischer will be kept intact, as well as historically significant items such as the Lucena, the Damiano, the first and second World Chess Championship contracts, 1886 and 1894, etc. The collection embodies the history of chess from its earliest days to the present, and I would like to see it continue along that path.' ∎

Youth Gone Wild

18-year-old Hans Niemann wins the World Open

How do you win the World Open? This is 2021 winner Hans Niemann, as he put it himself, 'drawing inspiration from the lions in the zoo'.

The World Open in Philadelphia has always been considered the granddaddy of American open tournaments. The 49th edition of Bill Goichberg's brainchild ended in an Armageddon tiebreak between John Burke and Hans Niemann that brought the latter 'all the privileges and honours that the title brings' plus a paycheque of $12,221.50. **HAROLD SCOTT**, who, together with Joel Benjamin, is writing a book on the rich and colourful history of the World Open, reports.

Many things have changed over the years at the World Open, which was first organized by Bill Goichberg's Continental Chess Association in New York in 1973 and has been almost exclusively held in Philadelphia since 1977. There were early American successes for names like Browne, Fedorowicz, Gurevich, Benjamin, Christiansen, Rohde, De Firmian and Dlugy. Then came the collapse of the Iron Curtain and a new crop of players would come to dominate the World Open in the nineties. Players like Yermolinsky, Shabalov, Goldin, Kaidanov and Kamsky would bring their unique personalities and approaches to the game, forever changing the landscape of chess in the United States.

After the turn of the Millennium, we had another group of players that had continued success in the World Open, such as Ehlvest, Yudasin, Nakamura, Onischuk, Najer and Akobian. In recent years, the tournament has seen success coming from the college ranks – particularly Illya Nyzhnyk, who is a graduate of Webster University in St. Louis. Illya is a four-time first-place finisher in the World Open. In fact, he would prove to be a factor again in this year's Open.

John van Neumann

The World Open has seen its share of cheating scandals over the years. In *Winning the World Open*, the book that Joel Benjamin and I have been writing over the past six months and that will be published later this year, we cover them all in detail.

In 1993, there was a player by the name of John von Neumann, which was coincidentally the same name as a famous Hungarian-American mathematician. This was the earliest case of computer cheating in chess. It is a very odd tale, as the lines of communication between Mr. von Neumann and his accomplice often were down. In one game, after nine moves were played, he sat there and waited for his flag to fall.

In 2006, there were two well-known cases of cheating at the World Open. In one case, a player had a device that he claimed was a hearing aid. However, an alert director exercised additional due diligence and discovered that it was a device known as a 'Phonito'. This was a transmission capable device which could be used to receive moves from an accomplice. The second case involved a man by the name of Eugene Varshavsky. He wore a big drooping hat that covered his ears. He flew relatively under the radar until Round 7. In that round, he faced world-class player Ilya Smirin and was victorious. The quality of his moves was extremely high, and when asked to play without his hat in the subsequent rounds, well let's just say he played about 1000 points weaker.

The World Open is Bill Goichberg's brainchild. For the first time in 49 years he was absent, as his wife Brenda was ill.

Over 1,000 players

This year the annual pilgrimage to Philadelphia for the World Open was special for many reasons. Last year the World Open was forced online due to the pandemic. However, in 2021 it was back to over-the-board, with many of its participants feeling grateful for some semblance of

For many this was a reunion of friends who had not seen each other for the better part of a year and a half

normalcy. As you might expect, for many this was a reunion of friends who had not seen each other for the better part of a year and a half. Unfortunately, for the first time in the history of the World Open Bill Goichberg was noticeably absent, as his wife Brenda was ill. Brenda has been a fixture at chess control for many years at the World Open, and I wish her well and hope she will be back for next year's 50th Anniversary tournament.

Over 1,000 players registered for this year's main event, with 193 players in the Open Section. Protocols were in place against the continued threat of Covid for such a large gathering. Temperature checks were done at the entrance to the playing hall and players, spectators and staff were all required to wear masks. Refusal to wear a mask would result in expulsion from the tournament. Fortunately, no one failed the temperature check test and no one outright refused to wear a mask. Directors would often have to remind players to have their mask on or to extend it to cover their nose. For practically all players, this was not a problem when receiving the reminder. As a tournament director myself, I had to remind one player in particular to cover his nose with his mask. He proceeded to call me an [expletive] as he argued that his nose was covered. At which time, I simply adjusted his clock with a penalty of 20 minutes. After which, he said, 'Is that the [expletive] deduction?' I then warned him that any further profanity would result in a forfeit loss. Strangely enough, I never heard from him again throughout the tournament. This was a rare case, as most cheerfully 'masked up' after they realized they mistakenly were not in compliance.

The always colourful Fed

There were a couple noticeable absences. Alexander Shabalov, a five-time first-place finisher, was on vacation in the American state of Georgia. Alex was busy enjoying some downtime after playing in the Chicago Open and National Open recently. I also suspect he is doing some preparation for the upcoming U.S. Senior Championship in St. Louis. The other player that I would expect to see at the World Open is Varuzhan Akobian. He is a 'four-timer' at the World Open and would have to be considered among the favourites. However, the always colourful John 'Fed' Fedorowicz did play again after an outstanding result in the 2019 edition. This year, the 62-year-old Fed turned in another solid result scoring an undefeated 6/9. For his efforts, Fed would pocket about $1400 and he proved that his fighting spirit continues to burn strongly. Here is a third-round victory of John's that had an interesting finish to it.

Jose Manuel Dominguez (2181)
John Fedorowicz (2413)
Philadelphia World Open 2021 (3)

position after 20.♖d7

**20...♗xf3 21.♕xf3 ♕xc4
22.♖xe7?**
Stronger was 22.b3 ♕h4 23.g3 ♕g5 24.h4 ♕f5 25.♕xf5 exf5 26.♖xe7 ♖fe8 27.♖c7 ♖ac8 28.♖a7 ♖e6, when nevertheless Black is much better and should be able to cash in the point without much of a problem.
22...♕h4

An unusual double attack that finishes things immediately.
0-1.

Cracking the 2600 barrier

This year's champion 18-year-old Hans Niemann has been on an incredible run in 2021. In January, he became a newly-minted Grandmaster. In June, he was a graduating senior at Columbia Grammar Preparatory School on New York City's Upper West Side. Despite the pandemic, Hans was able to thrive. Classes at CGPS were done remotely, which enabled him to travel around Europe and play. He has been in contention at the recent Chicago and National Opens. He also tied for first place in the Philadelphia International, which ran back-to-back with the World Open. His Elo has climbed rapidly, having started the year at 2484 and now cracking the 2600 barrier for the first time.

The tournament began very well for Hans, by scoring 4½ in the first five rounds. In Round 6, Niemann kicked things into second gear scoring an impressive win over the tournament's top-seed Jeffery Xiong. This was also Hans' first victory over a player rated 2700+.

NOTES BY
Hans Niemann

**Jeffery Xiong
Hans Niemann**
Philadelphia World Open 2021 (6)
Closed Catalan

It's the 6th round and I had 4½/5. I hadn't really played too many strong players yet, 2370 being my highest opponent. I drew my 3rd round, which some could argue is a delayed Swiss gambit but it clearly worked out. I wasn't sure who I was going to play but when I got my pairing against Jeffery Xiong I wasn't sure how to feel. This would be the highest rated opponent I've played OTB, but I was excited for the opportunity.
1.d4 ♘f6 2.c4 e6 3.g3

Xiong opts for the Catalan but plays g3 first. The point is to prevent the Queen's Indian, as ...b6 would allow ♗g2 with tempo. I had a tough decision to make here. The g3 move order allows for ...c5, which can transpose into a Benoni. 3.g3 is definitely not a challenging variation against the Benoni so I was tempted to make things interesting. However, I played ...c5 in multiple games recently and didn't want to fall into any preparation.
3...d5 4.♗g2 ♗b4+ 5.♗d2 ♗e7
The idea of ...♗b4+ is to provoke ♗d2 which has several drawbacks for White. The bishop would ideally go to b2 and now must go to c3 to occupy the a1-h8 diagonal, however the c3-square is meant for the knight.
6.♘f3 0-0 7.0-0 c6 8.♕c2 ♘bd7

9.♖d1 b6 10.♗f4 ♗b7 11.♘e5

This is still well known and I was still very comfortable. I was a bit surprised that he went for this line as Black can equalize pretty easily.

11...♘h5 12.♗d2 ♘hf6 13.cxd5 cxd5 14.♘c6 ♗xc6 15.♕xc6

White gains the bishop pair, but loses a few tempi in the process. In the short term, Black will have some initiative and be totally equal. However, the bishop on g2 can create havoc on the light squares long-term.

15...a6

Taking away the b5-square so the queen must retreat to a4 after ...♖c8 or ...♕c8.

16.♕c2 ♕c8 17.♕d3 b5 18.♖c1 ♕b7 19.♘c3 b4 20.♘a4

I was feeling very good here and perhaps my confidence got the best of me. The most logical move is to simply play 20...♖fc8, and it's definitely the best move. Maybe it was the nerves or the excitement. But I went for complications with 20...♕b5. The computer hates it, but I don't think it is that bad from a practical perspective.

20...♕b5 21.♘c5 ♘xc5 22.dxc5

Jeffery Xiong's wish to win at all cost against Hans Niemann was certainly laudable, but his efforts ended in a loss.

♖fb8 23.c6 ♖c8 24.♖c2 ♘g4

...♘e5 is a threat and I started to feel like the c6-pawn was becoming more of a weakness than an asset. White's biggest problem is the bishop on g2 and I felt that if the bishop's diagonal didn't open up then I'd always be fine.

25.♕xb5 25.♕d4 is the engine's top choice and apparently I'm in trouble. I thought that I might be able to take on e2 but I was sorely mistaken as ♗c3 ends the game on the spot. I would be forced to play 25...h5 and my position would be very bad. This was Xiong's only opportunity to secure a winning advantage.

25...axb5 26.e4

I was very surprised by this but

I started to get the feeling that Xiong really wanted to win this game. At multiple moments he chose the most aggressive possibility, which gave me chances for an advantage.

26...b3 27.♖cc1 dxe4

28.axb3 28.♗xe4 was a possibility, but I was going to take on a2 and I felt that I could blockade the bishop with the knight on d5. Additionally, the rook on a1 is pretty stuck and it's hard for White to attack the b1-pawn, while attacking the c6-pawn is not very difficult.

28...♖xa1 29.♖xa1 f5 I felt like the tables were turning and he started to get low on time as 40 moves approached.

NIC Interactive eBooks

Enjoy the advantages of a NIC Interactive eBook on your PC, notebook, smartphone or tablet: it's an exact copy of the printed book, it arrives within a couple of minutes, the postman will not be ringing your doorbell, it doesn't take up space on your bookshelves, and it allows you to replay all the games and variations on the built-in chessboard.

30.♖c1 ♘e5 31.c7 I played a bit too quickly here and I feel like I should have been more precise. It's clear that Black is better but the c-pawn is dangerous and the g2-bishop can come into the game and cause havoc. My next move, 31...♗d6, was definitely a bit sloppy, as 31...♘d3 would have solidified a clear advantage.

31...♗d6 After 31...♘d3 32.♖c6 ♔f7 the point is that 33.♗a5 is met with 33...♗b4 34.♗b6. Black has time to bring his king in and it's very hard for White to defend: 34...♔e7 35.♗f1 ♗d6 36.♖c3 ♘b4 37.♗xb5 ♘d5 38.♖c6 ♘xb6 39.♖xb6 ♖xc7 40.♗c4, with good winning chances for Black.
32.♗a5 ♔f7 33.♗f1 ♘f3+ 34.♔g2 ♘d4 35.♗b6 e5 36.f4

Another key moment where Xiong showed that he wanted to win at all cost. Objectively it's not a terrible move, but again he's giving me chances.
36...exf3+ 37.♔f2 ♘e6 38.♔xf3 ♗xc7 39.b4
I'm sort of in zugzwang so I just decided to push my kingside pawns and wait to see what he does with the pin.

39...g5 40.♔g2 h5 41.♖c6 g4 42.♗c5 This allows me to untangle yet again. The computer still says it's equal, but I get to activate my pieces and create more chances. His time was starting to get low so I felt an opportunity to win was near.
42...♖b8 43.♗d3 e4 44.♗c2 ♗e5 45.♗b3 ♖e8 46.♗e3 ♔f6 47.♖b6 h4

If White does absolutely nothing and moves back and forth then I actually can't make progress. I could pick up the b2-pawn but even then I'm sort of in zugzwang. Anyways, it's hard for White to sit, and Xiong wanted to win so he took the pawn on b5. But his ambition cost him the game.
48.♖xb5 h3+ 49.♔f2 f4 50.gxf4 ♘xf4 51.♖b7

This was the final mistake and I calculated a forced win.
51...♘e6 Forcing the reply: **52.♔g1 ♗d4** This is the simplest way to win. The h-pawn will simply queen.
53.♔f2 g3+ Taking advantage of the king not being able to recapture, and forcing 54.hxg3.
54.hxg3 ♖h8

There's nothing White can do about the threat of ...h2. The e4-pawn is key, as it prevents the bishop from attacking h1.
55.♗c2 ♗xe3+ 56.♔xe3 ♘g5 57.♖b6+ ♔e7 White's checks won't achieve anything. The h-pawn is unstoppable and the game is over. White resigned.

■ ■ ■

Niemann continued with the following quick win against Benjamin Gledura, the strong young grandmaster from Hungary.

NOTES BY
Joel Benjamin

Hans Niemann
Benjamin Gledura
Philadelphia World Open 2021 (7)
Neo-Grünfeld Defence

1.d4 ♘f6 2.c4 g6 3.f3 d5 4.cxd5 ♘xd5 5.e4 ♘b6 6.♘c3 ♗g7 7.♗e3 0-0 8.♕d2 ♘c6 9.0-0-0 f5 10.e5 f4 This sacrifice is a relatively recent attempt to increase Black's piece activity. 10...♘b4 was once seen exclusively in practice.

Benjamin Gledura was also too optimistic in his desire to beat Hans Niemann.

11. ♗xf4

With youthful confidence, Niemann grabs the pawn. 11.♗f2 ♘b4 12.a3 a5 13.h4 ♗e6 14.♘h3 ♘a2+ 15.♘xa2 ♗xa2 was seen in So-Carlsen, Stavanger 2019, when Wesley uncorked the strange 16.d5?! and managed a draw with great difficulty.

11...♗e6 11...♘b4 was seen in two previous games. Gledura's move looks a bit more accurate, to maintain pressure on d4, as 12.♗h6? ♕xd4 is not an option. Also, Black can do without the move ...a7-a5.

12. ♗e3 ♘b4 13.a3 ♘a2+

Following Carlsen's lead, but 13...♘4d5 is a reasonable option.

14.♘xa2 ♗xa2 15.♗d3

15...c5?

It's so tempting to try to take advantage of White's king stuck on the c-file, but this simply doesn't work. Maybe Gledura was surprised by White's last move. Black had a variety of sensible moves, e.g. 15...♘c4 with a typically unclear position.

16.dxc5 ♗xe5? This of course compounds the error, but otherwise Black's previous move had no point.

17.cxb6 ♖c8+ 18.♗c2 ♗b3

The problem for Black is that his 'threat' to capture on c2 is actually an optical illusion.

19.♘e2! ♕d6 Neither capture recoups material: 19...♖xc2+ 20.♕xc2, or 19...♗xc2 20.♕xd8 ♗xd1+ 21.♕xc8 ♖xc8+ 22.♔xd1.

20.♘c3 ♖xc3 21.♕xc3! 1-0.

■ ■ ■

Illya Nyzhnyk is a very dangerous player in open tournaments and has finished atop the leaderboard in four of five World Opens from 2014-2018. After 7 rounds, Nyzhnyk looked like he was in position for another victory at the World Open. In Round 8, he

would have the white pieces against Niemann. Just two weeks prior, in the National Open, Nyzhnyk had defeated him with Black in the final round to earn a five-way share of first. Would history repeat itself? Well, Hans was able to hold Illya to a draw. Entering the final round, it was likely that Illya would need a win to join the winner's group, as Niemann would require only a draw to clinch at least a tie for first. Standing in Illya's way was John Burke, who took the point home for a share of first.

John Burke is known for becoming the youngest player to reach an Elo rating of 2600, in 2015 at the age of 14.

John's tournament started off well, with three wins in a row. But then came a pivotal Round 4 game against top seed Jeffery Xiong. John achieved a winning position. However, Jeffery was able to complicate the game just enough for John to slip up.

After this setback, John did manage to regroup, and he won his next two games. After 8 rounds he was in striking distance with 6½ points, but would need a win against Illya Nyzhnyk. Here is their final-round encounter that would propel John into a tie for first with Niemann.

NOTES BY
John Burke

John Burke
Illya Nyzhnyk
Philadelphia World Open 2021 (9)
Petroff Defence, Marshall Variation

Illya is my former teammate at Webster University and I've roomed with him in a couple of previous tournaments, so I'm very well acquainted with his approach to chess. He has a knack for almost always finding a way to win open tournaments, and at the time he had not lost a classical game in two years. Granted, that's partly thanks to the pandemic, but still! He plays a bunch of openings, so I didn't do too much deep preparation. I just intended to play what I know best and try to steer toward a two-result game if possible. He also tends to be a very quick player, so I made sure to remember to stick close to him on the clock as well.

1.e4 e5 This is a sign that he's probably going to play the Petroff. In a previous game against him in 2019 I avoided it with 2.♗c4, but failed to cause him serious problems.

2.♘f3 ♘f6 It might seem like this is a surprising opening choice on his part, given that he needs a win to have a shot at tournament victory, but a draw would still give both of us a very decent prize haul. Also, his live rating before this game was a peak of 2689, so perhaps he wanted to protect that in his quest to reach 2700.

3.♘xe5 d6 4.♘f3 ♘xe4 5.d4 d5 6.♗d3 ♗d6

There are a few different ways to play for Black here, but I knew that he favours the ultra-solid 6...♗d6 system. I didn't check this before the game, but in fact I had briefly reviewed my notes a few rounds prior, when I thought I might be playing him with the same colours.

7.0-0 0-0 8.c4 c6 9.♖e1

This is one of the main lines, but it's not as popular as 9.♘c3, which most people play nowadays. He must not have been as familiar with this move, as he began to think here.

9...♗b4?

This is already a serious inaccuracy. I probably retain a nice edge even with a simple move like 10.♖e2, but there's a more direct way of playing.

John Burke knew he had to stay alert till the very end if he wanted to defeat his former team and roommate Ilya Nyzhnyk.

Black should simply have defended the knight with 9...♖e8 or 9...♗f5.

10.♘c3!

This is possible due to various tactics involving ♗xh7+. I knew that this position must be pretty nice for me, since I was confident that 9...♗b4 was not the correct move. But, I didn't suspect just *how* bad it is for Black.

10...♗xc3

Once you play 9...♗b4, it's natural to attempt to justify it by going in for a direct continuation.

With the extra ♘c3 tempo being gifted to me, he can't switch back to

defending his knight with 10...♗f5, after which White goes 11.♕b3. The bishop just doesn't belong on b4. Very often Black plays ...♘a6 in this line, with ...♘b4 ideas, but now I'm several tempi up on the main lines: 10...♘xc3 11.bxc3 ♗xc3? 12.♗xh7+

ANALYSIS DIAGRAM

12...♔xh7 (12...♔h8 looks insanely risky. I admit that I didn't figure everything out in advance, but I was sure that this must be good for White, and I was also sure that he would never go for it: 13.♗g5! f6 14.♗c2 fxg5 15.♘e5 g4 16.♘g6+ ♔g8 17.♘e7+ ♔h8 18.♖e5 winning)

13.♕d3+ (the problem for Black isn't necessarily that I win the bishop back, it's more important that his king is tremendously weak) 13...♔g8

ANALYSIS DIAGRAM

14.♘g5! (including this move first induces further weaknesses) 14...g6 15.♕xc3, winning.

11.bxc3 ♘xc3 12.♕c2 ♘e4 13.♗xe4 dxe4 14.♕xe4

If he had time to play a couple moves in a row, he might be able to stabilize, but I'm just too far ahead in development. Not only is ♘g5 an idea, I also have the annoying threat of ♗a3, winning the exchange.

14...♘d7 15.♗a3 ♘f6

He played this quickly, so I have to wonder if he simply missed my next move.

15...c5 is not pretty, but at least I don't have an immediate win here, and he can try to hang on.

16.♕e7

Other queen moves would still leave me with a pleasant position, but it would give him a chance to develop. But this is just a straightforward forcing solution that forces a transition to a completely winning endgame.

16...♖e8 17.♕xd8 ♖xd8 18.♗e7 ♖d7

I was even wondering if he would sacrifice an exchange with 18...♗e6, but of course this isn't really an improvement on the game continuation: 19.♗xd8 ♖xd8 20.♘e5 ♖xd4 21.♖ab1 and White is winning.

19.♗xf6 gxf6 20.♖e8+ ♔g7

I should act immediately while he

still has two moves to play (...b6 and ...♗b7) to untangle.

21.♘h4 My threat is ♘f5+ followed by ♘e7+, so he has to shed a pawn to make room for his king.

21...f5 21...♖xd4 22.♖xc8 ♖xc8 23.♘f5+ and wins.

22.♘xf5+ ♔f6 23.g4 b6

All my moves up to this point have been pretty straightforward, but now I took a decent think to make sure I converted smoothly. I have everything I could possibly want here, but Illya is such a resourceful player, and I've seen him perform some incredible escapes from bad positions.

24.♖h8

This is the most incisive way. Either he gives me another pawn, or he puts his king on a bad square.

24...♗b7

I expected 24...♔g6, when I have my choice of wins. Here's one of them: 25.♖g8+ ♔f6 26.♘h6 ♗b7 (26...♖xd4 27.♖e1 winning) 27.g5+ ♔e7 28.♖e1+ ♔d6 29.♖g7 and White wins.

25.♖xh7 It's not only about winning a second pawn, his king is going to be in a mating net too.

25...♖g8 26.h3 c5

	Philadelphia World Open 2021				
					prize
1	Hans Niemann	2571	USA	7½	$12221.50
2	John Burke	2538	USA	7½	$11827.50
3	Jeffery Xiong	2709	USA	7	$2267.25
4	Jianchao Zhou	2603	CHN	7	$2267.25
5	Aram Hakobyan	2603	ARM	7	$2267.25
6	Andrew Zhang Hong	2474	USA	7	$2267.25
7	Illya Nyzhnyk	2683	UKR	6½	$349.29
8	Benjamin Gledura	2629	HUN	6½	$349.29
9	Vladimir Akopian	2625	USA	6½	$349.29
10	Zaven Andriasian	2581	ARM	6½	$349.29
11	Cemil Can Ali Marandi	2543	TUR	6½	$349.29
12	Pablo Salinas Herrera	2514	CHI	6½	$349.29
13	Vladimir Belous	2487	RUS	6½	$349.29
14	Brian Escalante	2440	PER	6½	$1500.00
15	Aleksandr Lenderman	2624	USA	6	
16	Timur Gareyev	2596	USA	6	
17	Nikolas Theodorou	2584	GRE	6	
18	Ehsan Ghaem-Maghami	2547	IRI	6	
19	Akshat Chandra	2530	USA	6	
20	Praveen Balakrishnan	2507	USA	6	
21	Christopher Repka	2503	SVK	6	
22	Atulya Arya Shetty	2453	USA	6	
23	Kassa Korley	2435	DEN	6	$1399.25
24	John Fedorowicz	2413	USA	6	$1399.25
25	Alexander Ross Katz	2405	USA	6	$1399.25
26	Jason Wang	2324	USA	6	$1399.25
27	Aaron Jacobson	2293	USA	6	$1500.00
28	Eddy Tian	2226	USA	6	$3943.00

In the Armageddon tiebreak Hans Niemann, as Black, had draw odds against John Burke, but with pointed play he even won.

Now I took my time to check things over and calculate to the end. It's never too late to throw away the win, so I made sure to slow down and confirm that he has no miracle defence.

27.d5 b5 28.f4 I'm giving away my pawns to execute his king. **28...bxc4 29.♖e1 c3** If 29...♖xd5 30.♘e7 and wins; 29...♗xd5 30.♖e5 ♖g6 31.♘g3 ♗e6 32.♘e4+ ♔e7 33.f5 winning. **30.♖e5** My threat is ♖h6+ followed by g5 mate. **30...♖g6 31.♘g3** ♘h5+ comes next, and there's no good way to parry it, so he resigned. For instance 31...♖g8 32.♘h5+ ♔g6 33.♖g5+ ♔xh7 34.♘f6+ ♔h6 35.♖xg8, winning.

■ ■ ■

It would come down to an Armageddon game to decide who was the 'official' champion of the 49th World Open. John Burke would have five

minutes on his clock and the white pieces. Hans Niemann would have four minutes and draw odds with the black pieces. Here is the game that would determine who would be 'receiving all the honours and privileges the title brings' as Alex Yermolinsky once said jokingly. However, it was worth almost an additional $500 for Niemann, with Niemann earning $12,221.50 and Burke earning $11,827.50. It should be said that somewhere around move 10 Hans offered John a draw, which drew laughs from the crowd as well as from Burke himself.

John Burke
Hans Niemann
Philadelphia World Open 2021
(Armageddon)
(notes by Joel Benjamin)

position after 28...♘c5

29.♘gf5
Niemann has played an excellent Armageddon game, staying solid while maintaining activity. Burke could perhaps present more problems by throwing the other knight in, 29.♘ef5. Still, there's nothing after 29...♖xd1 (29...♗f8 30.♘d4 exd4 31.♗xf6 d3! might do the job, too) 30.♖xd1 ♗f8! (the engine says 30...gxf5 31.exf5 e4 is equal, but why even look that way?).
29...♖xd1 30.♖xd1

30...♘cxe4!
Even easier than 30...♗f8.
31.♘xe7+ ♖xe7 32.♖d8+ ♔g7 33.♕d1 ♘xg5 34.hxg5 ♘e4 35.f3 ♘xg5 36.♖d6
The queen is almost trapped, but this isn't horseshoes.
36...♕c8 37.♕xb3 ♕c7 38.♕d1 ♘e6 39.♖d2 ♕b6 40.♕e1 e4!

With confident play, Hans wraps up the title.
41.fxe4 ♘g5 42.♔h1 ♘xe4 43.♖d4 ♕c7 44.♔g1 ♕e5 45.♘f1 c5 46.♖d8 c4 47.♘e3 ♘c5 48.♖d5 ♕xd5
0-1. ■

MAXIMize
your Tactics
with Maxim Notkin

Find the best move in the positions below

Solutions on page 95

1. Black to play

2. White to play

3. White to play

4. Black to play

5. White to play

6. Black to play

7. Black to play

8. Black to play

9. Black to play

THE WOMEN'S

GRAND PRIX

4th Stage
GIBRALTAR

Winner:

Zhansaya Abdumalik
Kazakhstan

Congratulations!

HM Government
of Gibraltar

www.gibchess.com

Judit Polgar

Many-sided Magnus Carlsen

He is incredibly strong and always on the alert to grab his chances. And he is uncannily cold-blooded when the heat is on. Fortunately, he is also human. **JUDIT POLGAR** looks at the lessons she learned from the current World Champion.

After finishing one of my games during the Benidorm 2003 rapid tournament, I started following with interest a time-scramble in another game. One of the players under time-pressure was a very young boy. Noticing my interest, Norwegian grandmaster Simen Agdestein, who was standing next to me, whispered a name into my ear: 'Magnus Carlsen'. He quickly added, 'You will be hearing about him a lot...'

The first time I had the opportunity to watch Magnus more closely and for a longer time was during the 2005 Wijk aan Zee tournament. It was my first appearance after the birth of my son Oliver, and following 14 months of competitive inactivity. Magnus was playing in the B-Group, fighting in the same area as the elite tournament. Still a boy, he was drinking orange juice and eating nuts from a big box with apparent fervour. It was obvious that he was not playing a part – this was Magnus. It goes without saying that he was playing very well already.

A few years later, many expected him to become World Champion one day. He was spending most of his time and energy on polishing his game and feeding his curiosity for chess knowledge. More than anything, he loved winning!

Trademark 1 – Pragmatism
Magnus always looks for the option that offers him the best chances of success, without any unnecessary complications. We can see this in both his away-from-the-board and his over-the-board decisions.

The final games from his most recent world title matches bear this out nicely. In his match against Sergey Karjakin in New York 2016, he did not try to use his final White game to win the match outright. Instead, Magnus preferred to make an eventless draw, confident that he would outclass his opponent in the rapid play-off. Something similar happened two years later, in his match against Fabiano Caruana in London. Magnus offered a draw after establishing a stable advantage as Black in their final game. In both cases, the results of the play-offs proved him right.

Magnus has his own unique way of keeping control of his games, and not allowing his opponents to create the desired counterplay. I could feel this during the following game:

Magnus Carlsen
Judit Polgar
Kristiansund 2010

position after 11.a4

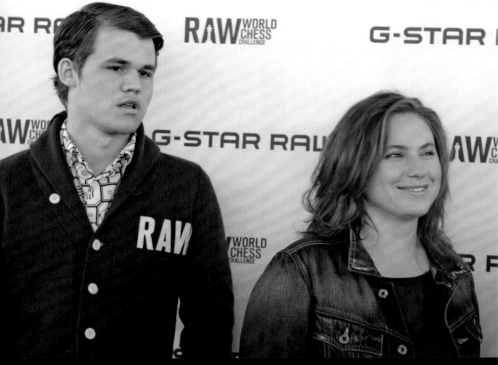

Magnus Carlsen and Judit Polgar at a G-Star fashion event in New York in 2010.

Trademark 2 – Alertness

Magnus maintains his focus at a consistent level throughout his games, remaining alert to his opponents' tiniest mistakes. He never misses a chance if it comes his way, as I found out in the next two games:

Magnus Carlsen
Judit Polgar
Mexico City rapid 2012 (3)

position after 18.♗d2

Things had rather gone my way, and had I played 18...♖b3, Magnus would still have had to prove his compensation for the pawn. Instead, I played the seemingly active:

18...♖c2? Carlsen's reply hit me like a cold shower: **19.♗b4!** Not only retrieving the pawn by force, but also simplifying to a better endgame.

19...♖xe2 20.♗xc5 ♖xe1+ 21.♖xe1 Now and two moves later, the unfortunate knight's placement causes me problems.

21...♖e8 22.♗xa7 ♖a8 23.♗c5 ♘c8 24.exd5 cxd5 25.♘xe5 ♖xa4

Magnus played **26.d4**, retaining the more pleasant position and eventu-

---

In view of the threat of a4-a5 (and if ...b6-b5, then a5-a6), I did not find castling queenside very appealing. At the same time, the pressure on g7 seems to make it hard for me to complete my kingside development. But I found the imaginative:

11...♗e7

My idea was to meet 12.♗xg7? with 12...♖g8 13.♗f6 (forced if White wants to avoid ...♘h4) 13...♕f4! (an elegant and effective trick. Due to his hanging pieces, White suffers structural damage) 14.♗xe7 (14.♕xf4 is

Magnus has his unique way of keeping things under control, without allowing the opponent to reach the desired counterplay

no improvement: 14...♘xf4 15.♗xe7 ♖xg2+ 16.♔h1 ♔xe7, with a winning position) 14...♕xf3 15.gxf3 ♔xe7. White has won a pawn, but the kingside weaknesses leave him in a difficult position.

Magnus sensed the danger and reacted with the solid:

12.♕g3!!

Due to the hanging pawn on g7, I now had to exchange the queens, weakening the defence of my b6-pawn.

12...♕xg3 13.hxg3 0-0 14.a5! b5 15.a6! ♗c6 16.♘a5

White has achieved a considerable advantage, but I eventually managed to reach a draw (½-½, 108).

ally winning (1-0, 44). 26.♞c6 was also worth considering. In view of the threat ♜e8+, I would have had to exchange rooks with 26...♜a1 27.♜xa1 ♝xa1, when 28.♞b4 would have won a pawn.

Here I got into trouble because of my lack of tactical awareness. Spotting my mistake in the following game required a subtler understanding.

Magnus Carlsen
Judit Polgar
London 2012

position after 22.♜ed1

I did not have any special problems in this Hedgehog type of position, featuring some unusual knight placements on f8 and d2.

22...g6? If I had played a neutral move like 22...a6, the play would have continued in the spirit of the Hedgehog, with slow manoeuvring and prophylactic moves. The difference is that after 23.e5 dxe5 24.fxe5

ANALYSIS DIAGRAM

my f6-square would not be weak and the g6-square would be available for my reserve knight: 24...♞g6 25.♝xb7

Interviewing Magnus Carlsen at Norway Chess 2019. After she retired from professional chess, Judit Polgar became a popular commentator.

♛xb7 26.♞f3 ♜ed8!?, followed by either ...a6-a5 or ...h7-h5, with good counterplay.

I had thought that my last move was 'neutral enough', but Magnus's answer proved me wrong.

23.e5! I must confess that I just had not seen this move.

23...♝c6 Trying to keep the tension. In the event of 23...♝xf3 24.♞xf3 dxe5 25.fxe5, my f8-knight would be passive, and the threat of ♞e4, targeting f6, would be as unpleasant as it was later on in the game.

23...dxe5 24.fxe5 does not change much. Due to the hanging bishop on b7, I could not take on e5.

24.♝d4 ♜ed8 25.♝xc6 ♜xc6 26.♞f3 dxe5 27.fxe5 ♜dc8 28.♞e4 At this stage, Magnus had consolidated his advantage and he eventually won (1-0, 53).

Trademark 3 – Cold-bloodedness

Magnus has the ability to remain cold-blooded in dangerous positions. His unwavering self-confidence in any kind of situation can have a psychological effect on his opponent, too. This may be one of the reasons why there have been times when he played the Dragon Sicilian quite often.

Judit Polgar
Magnus Carlsen
Mainz rapid 2008

position after 20...♛a5

After spoiling Black's kingside structure, White has the natural **21.f5**, which seems to cause Black major problems. As if completely unaware of what was happening on the kingside, Magnus continued his positional attack with:

21...♜fc8!

The cautious 21...♗e5 would actually have offered me active ideas: 22.f6 (22.♖hg1, preparing g5-g6 is also interesting) 22...e6 23.♘f3!?. By forcing the bishop swap, I would have avoided any trouble.

22.f6

It may seem that my attack will break through sooner than Black's. In the event of 22...exf6 23.gxf6 ♗xf6 24.♖hg1+ ♔h8 25.♖df1, Black would be lost. However, Magnus had anticipated the resolute advance of my f-pawn and prepared:

22...e5! Black continues to ignore my kingside threats and maintains the rhythm of his attack. The pawn on c2 is doomed now. Caught by surprise, I failed to find the best answer.

23.♘f5?

23.fxg7 would have offered White better chances to stay in the game: 23...exd4 24.♗xd4 ♖xc2 25.♕xc2 ♖xc2 26.♔xc2. Despite the exposed position of my king, the game position is not entirely clear, e.g. 26...♕xa2+?! 27.♗b2 ♗e6 28.♖d3 (threatening ♖a1) 28...♕a6 29.♗f6, and Black's king is in potential danger and he might be forced to go for a perpetual soon.

23...♗xf5 24.exf5 ♖xc2 25.♕xc2 ♖xc2 26.♔xc2 ♕xa2+ 27.♔d3 ♗f8 28.♖c1 d5 and Magnus won (0-1, 44).

Even the strongest players on our planet are human, though, and sometimes, Carlsen displays signs of weakness. If the position gets irrational, he may become vulnerable to tactical tricks.

If the position becomes irrational, Magnus can be vulnerable to tactical tricks

Magnus Carlsen
Judit Polgar
Mexico City rapid 2012 (1)

position after 23.♕xa5

Things had not gone my way in my beloved King's Indian. After stabilizing the kingside, Magnus had won a pawn on the other wing, and his advantage is indisputable. I decided to change the course of events with the resolute:

23...f5!? 24.gxf5 24.exf5 ♘f6, followed by ...d6-d5 or 24...e4, would have yielded me strong counterplay.

24...♕xh5 25.♖e1 ♘f6 26.♘d5 ♖a8 27.♕b4 ♖fd8

Optically, the position seems irrational, but White is under no real threat. Almost any neutral move would maintain his advantage.

28.f3? This apparently consolidating move offers me a hidden tactical turn.

28...♕h4! 29.♖c1 ♗xd5?!

I immediately spotted the winning idea, but did not carry it out in optimal form. Stronger was 29...♘4xd5! 30.cxd5 ♘xd5, winning a piece.

30.cxd5?!

White could have stayed in the game with 30.♗xf4 ♕xf4 31.cxd5 ♘xd5 32.♕c4. I had calculated 32...♕xd2, missing the saving 33.♖g2!.

I could have deviated with 32...♘f6 33.♕c2 d5, with a strong initiative, but the fight would still have been on.

30...♘4xd5

Due to the pin along the fourth rank, I won a piece and later the game. Magnus's 'desperado' did not change anything:

31.♗xg5 ♕xg5 32.♖xg5 ♘xb4 and I eventually won (0-1, 50).

Conclusions

■ Alertness is essential for being able to swoop down on your opponent's slightest mistake in both equal and worse positions.

■ One should remain cold-blooded no matter how complicated the position. ■

Thomas Willemze

What would you play?

Which pieces fit into your plans and which are rather a burden? That's a crucial question if you're considering to exchange a piece. Or not.

The ability to make the right exchange is an invaluable skill in chess. The key is to to identity the pieces that you want to spend the rest of the game with and to find the most effective way to get rid of the others.

Exercises

The game between Anna-Daria Marcu (1533) and Lia Alexandra Maria (1713) from the Romanian Women's Championship was an interesting battle in which finding the correct way to trade pieces played an important role. I have selected four critical moments for White and turned them into exercises to enable you to improve your own decision-making skills.

Exercise 1

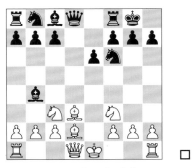

position after 8...0-0

White has sacrificed a pawn in return for rapid development and has to find a way to get compensation. What would you play? Would you quickly tuck away your king with **9.0-0**, prepare queenside castling with **9.♕e2**, or put your knight in the centre with the aggressive **9.♘e5**?

Exercise 2

position after 15...e5

With her last move, Black unintentionally created a tactical opportunity for her opponent. Can you find it? You can choose between **16.♘xf6+**, **16.♗xe5**, and **16.♗xh6**.

Exercise 3

position after 19...♔h8

White has played well so far, but needs a precise follow-up. Would you recapture the piece with **20.♗xd7**, eliminate the defending bishop with **20.♗e4**, or ignore the knight for the moment and continue your attack with **20.♕h3**?

Exercise 4

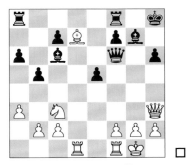

position after 21...♕f6

White has restored the material balance and is facing an important decision. Would you trade bishops with **22.♗xc6**, activate your knight with **22.♘d5**, or open up the f-file for your rook with **22.f4**?

I hope you enjoyed these exercises and were able to pinpoint the moments at which White could have demonstrated her piece-trading skills. You can find the full analysis of this game on the following pages.

An interesting battle in which finding the correct way to trade pieces played an important role

Anna-Daria Marcu (1533)
Lia Alexandra Maria (1713)
Romanian Women's
Championship, Fano 2021
French Defence, Winawer Variation

**1.e4 e6 2.d4 d5 3.♘c3 ♗b4
4.♗d2 dxe4**

5.♘xe4 It is very common to sacrifice the d-pawn against the French Defence, but 5.♕g4! was required to

It is very common to sacrifice the d-pawn against the French Defence, but 5.♕g4! was required to get enough compensation

get enough compensation. The aim is to target the g7-pawn and get decent compensation after, for instance, 5...♕xd4 6.♘f3! ♕f6 7.♕xe4.
5...♕xd4

6.♘c3
This retreat was necessary to keep the b2-pawn safe. Note that 6.♗xb4?? loses a piece after 6...♕xe4+!, with a double attack.
6...♘f6 7.♘f3 ♕d8 8.♗d3 0-0

Black is in excellent shape. She is a pawn up and her rock-solid position will make it very hard for her opponent to find a target for creating counterplay.
9.0-0
This is the most solid answer to **Exercise 1**, but not a move that will discomfort her opponent. The most convincing try would be to go for opposite castling with 9.♕e2 and 10. 0-0-0 and set up a kingside attack.

The aggressive 9.♘e5 would be premature, because Black can easily expel the white knight from its dream square with 9...♘bd7!.
**9...♘bd7 10.a3 ♗e7 11.♗f4 a6
12.♕e2**
White continues to make healthy developing moves, hoping to generate counterplay later in the game.
12...b5 13.♖ad1 ♗b7

14.♘g5 The knight is not really

threatening anything, but will soon provoke a game-changing event.
14...h6

15.♘ge4 White is not powerful enough to successfully breach the enemy position. After 15.♘xe6 fxe6 16.♕xe6+ ♔h8 17.♕h3

ANALYSIS DIAGRAM

Black has several ways to neutralize the attack. The most convincing one is to bring in her best defender with 17...♕e8! 18.♗xh6 ♕h5!.
15...e5 This move weakens the light squares and allows a tactical combination. Black could have preserved her well-earned advantage with 15...♕c8 and 16...c5.

16.♘xf6+!

This move prepares a nice tactical combination and was the correct solution to **Exercise 2**.
16.♗xe5 gives Black way too much

18.♗h7+ ♘xh7 19.♖xd8 ♖axd8.
16...♗xf6
Black had no choice, since 16...♘xf6 17.♗h7+ ♘xh7 18.♖xd8 ♖axd8

Starting a combination with the sacrifice move has the drawback that your opponent can often defend by picking up the material and returning it later

material for the queen after 16...♘xe5 17.♘xf6+ ♗xf6 18.♗h7+ ♔xh7 19.♖xd8 ♖axd8.

16.♗xh6 is based on the same combination as in the game, but with the wrong move order! Starting a combination with the sacrifice move has the drawback that your opponent can often defend by picking up the material and returning it later.

ANALYSIS DIAGRAM

16...gxh6 17.♘xf6+ ♘xf6!. Black is already a piece up and can safely surrender the queen for a bishop and a rook. Black is clearly better after

19.♕xe5 gives Black only *one* bishop and a rook for the queen.
17.♗xh6! Well done!

17...gxh6
This move weakens the black king's position considerably. 17...♕e7 would have been the safer choice.
18.♗f5!
This was the point of the combination. The knight will soon be attacked by both the white bishop and the white queen. Remember that none of this would have happened with a black pawn still on e6.
18...♗c6 19.♕g4+ ♔h8

20.♕h3
This move leaves White on top, but was not the correct answer to **Exercise 3**. White probably wanted to remove the queen from the g-file, because she realized that 20.♗xd7 would run straight into 20...♖g8!. However, a much more effective way to neutralize this threat was by identifying the most important black piece and **trading it as quickly as possible** with 20.♗e4! ♗xe4 21.♘xe4.

ANALYSIS DIAGRAM

Please take your time to compare this diagram to the previous one and enjoy the progress that White made in only two moves! Simply by trading off one single piece. Suddenly, Black is powerless against moves like ♖xd7, ♕f5 and ♘g3-h5.

20...♗g7 21.♗xd7 ♕f6

We have arrived at **Exercise 4**.

22.♗xc6

White wants to trade these bishops, but should have effected this with 22.♘d5!. **If possible, always force your opponent to make the trade**. White will have an extra tempo compared to the game after 22...♗xd7 23.♕xd7 ♕g6.

The third option, 22.f4, opens up the f-file, but also considerably increases the black dark-squared bishop's elbow room. Black is slightly better after 22...exf4 23.♗xc6 ♕xc6 24.♖xf4 ♖ad8.

22...♕xc6 23.♕d7 ♕g6 24.♘d5 ♕xc2 25.♕xc7 ♕xb2

Black played very well during the last five moves and has created a difficult choice for her opponent. Should she defend her a-pawn to restrict Black's dangerous queenside pawns, or seek active counterplay?

26.♕a5

The queen belongs in the centre and feels very uncomfortable in such a passive role. The active 26.♘b6! ♖ae8

27.♘d7 ♖g8 28.♖d6 would have been the better choice.

ANALYSIS DIAGRAM

After 28...♕xa3 29.♕c6 White suddenly threatens mate in two with 30.♖xh6!. Black can defend with 29...♔h7, but after 30.♘f6+ ♗xf6 31.♖xf6 ♕f8 32.♖a1 White will be able to pick up the queenside pawns and equalize comfortably.

26...♕c2 27.♘b4 ♕g6

28.♖c1 This move wastes valuable time. The white knight and queen had to return to the centre as quickly as possible.

28...♖fd8 29.h3 e4 30.♖c6 ♖d6

31.♖fc1

White really needed her queen back

on the streets! 31.♕c7 would have been a better attempt, even though Black is still clearly in charge.

31...♗e5

The beautiful 31...e3, to weaken the dark squares, would have been even more convincing, as 32.fxe3 would run into 32...♕g5!.

ANALYSIS DIAGRAM

The point is that Black wins both rooks after 33.♖xd6 ♕xe3+ 34.♔h1 (34.♔f1 ♕xc1+ 35.♔f2 ♕c5+) 34...♕xc1+ 35.♔h2 ♕f4+ 36.g3 ♕xd6.

32.♖6c5 ♗f4 33.♖e1

33...e3 This powerful pawn move opens up the second rank by force and decides the game after all.

34.fxe3 ♖d2 35.g4 ♕e4

White resigned.

Conclusion

White fought hard in this game and could have rewarded herself by finding a more effective way to trade the right pieces. I hope this game has contributed to your own piece-trading skills and will help you to take the right decisions in your games! ■

MAXIMize your Tactics Solutions

1. Xiong-Tsydypov
Titled Tuesday 2021

40...♖c8! Three major pieces are en prise! But 41.♕xd5 and 41.♕xa6 fail to 41...♖xc1 mate, and 41.♕xc8 to 41...♕xa2 mate. White resigned.

2. Puranik-Minhazuddin
Bangladesh 2021

26.♕xg7+! Black resigned, as after 26...♔xg7 27.♖g5++ his choice is unenviable: 27...♔f7 28.♖g7 mate or 27...♔h6 28.♗g7 mate.

3. Sochacki-Rogule
European Online CC 2021

White rudely took the enemy king out of its comfort zone with **34.♕xf8+! ♔xf8 35.♖b8+ ♔e7 36.♖1b7** Mate.

4. Schroeder-Heimann
Hobbits Invitational 2021

One by one the black pieces jump from the rear, forcing liquidation into a winning endgame. **36...♕e1+! 37.♖xe1 ♖xe1+ 38.♔h2 ♗e5** White resigned.

5. Parvanyan-Manik
European Online CC 2021

The well-known blow **26.♕xh7+! ♔xh7 27.♖h5+** is seemingly parried by **27...♕h6**, but White has an extra resource: **28.♗d3+**, mating in three. Black resigned.

6. Khodko-Gutenev
Russia 2021

30...♕xb4! 31.cxb4 ♘d2+! 32.♖xd2 ♖a1+! 33.♔xa1 ♖c1 mate. 32...♖c1+! 33.♔xc1 ♖a1 mate, when the rook on d2 blocks the escape route, is equally beautiful.

7. He-Brunner
PNWCC Online Blitz 2021

The threats of 32.♕xg7 mate and 32.♕xe6+ are impossible to deal with, but, as they say, the best defence is offence: **31...♘e3+! 32.fxe3 ♖c2+ 33.♔h3 ♕f1+ 34.♔h4 ♖xh2+ 35.♔g5 h6+** White resigned in view of 36.♔g6 ♕f7 mate.

8. Fedoseev-Duda
European Online CC 2021

Black neatly disentangled with **24...♗c5+ 25.♔h2 ♗g1+!** Not 25...♕xb2+? 26.♕g2 or 26.♕e2. **26.♔xg1 ♕b6+ 27.♔h2 ♗xe4**. The only annoying detail is that he managed to lose this totally winning position.

9. Gokerkan-V.Kovalev
European Online CC 2021

39...♘f2! Not 39...♘g3? 40.♖xf4+ ♔h4 (40...♔g4 41.♖g7+) 41.♘g6+ ♔g4 42.♘e5+ ♔h4 43.♘f3+ or 42...♔f4 43.♘d3+. **40.♘xf4+** 40.g3 ♘g4+ 41.♔h3 (41.♔g2 ♖f2+ 42.♔g1 fxg3) 41...f3 and after a few checks the ...♖h1# threat is decisive. **40...♔g4 41.g3 ♔f3!** And Black won.

Jan Timman

Fifty Shades of Ray

'He has a great knack of putting a lively perspective on events.' **JAN TIMMAN** has always liked Raymond Keene's style of writing and enjoyed his latest book, a collection of shorter pieces and more essayistic articles on chess and its role in art, culture and civilisation.

Seventy-three-year-old English grandmaster Ray Keene has been an extremely productive chess writer all his life. An old memory: in the summer of 1975, I visited Keene after a tournament in the London district of Earls Court. He was still living in Acton then. We took the train to Brighton for a look at the Royal Pavilion. Back in London, we bought a replica of an 18-century gaming table, which ended up in my spacious room on the Weteringschans in Amsterdam. At the time, Keene told me that he had 48 books to his name so far – that's how I remember it, anyway. I was impressed – I hadn't even published one yet. Keene sometimes wrote a book in two weeks, but not always. *Aron Nimzowitsch: A Reappraisal* had taken him months. The book got a good reception, and was even translated into Russian.

I have always liked Keene's style of writing. He has a great knack of putting a lively perspective on events, a good example being *Karpov-Korchnoi 1978. The Inside Story of the Match*. Judiciously, and with dry, understated humour, he describes the bizarre events taking place during the match: the trouble with the Ananda Marga cult, the yoghurt incident he

Keene sometimes wrote a book in two weeks, but not always

had caused himself, Petra Leeuwerik's shenanigans and the scheming of the mysterious Dr. Zukhar. The publication of the book angered Kortchnoi, because Keene had signed a contract forbidding him, as Kortchnoi's second, to work on a book during the match. It caused a lot of ruckus – far too much as far as I am concerned. Keene's book was light-footed, little more than glorified diary entries. Who can object to

someone keeping a diary? Everything indicated that Keene had discharged his job satisfactorily.

Later, Keene wrote several more books about world championship matches, none of them a match for *The Inside Story*.

Plagiarism

If you write a lot, you will inevitably experience the unpleasant pressure of the deadline. I know two excellent and successful Dutch authors who succumbed to it by committing plagiarism. The same thing happened to Keene, and he was severely taken to task for it on some websites. In his case, it was probably not only due to deadlines. Providing dry technical commentary to chess games is just not his forte, and he doesn't seem very interested in it, evincing a clear preference for more philosophical exposés, as in his book about Nimzowitsch.

Keene wrote for *The Times* and *The Spectator* for over three decades, and I often had the feeling that he felt constricted by the limited leeway allowed him there. I feel the same about Hans Ree's weekly column in the Dutch newspaper *NRC Handelsblad*. Good writers should have no restrictions. Keene has been writing for the online platform *The Article* of late, where he enjoys room to expatiate.

Donner in Venice

Now he has collected 50 pieces in a book entitled *Fifty Shades of Ray*, published by Hardinge Simpole. It's sub-titled *Chess in the year of the Coronavirus Pandemic*, and also contains articles from *British Chess Magazine*, although I much prefer his essayistic pieces from *The Article*.

In his Introduction, Keene writes: '... I have found inspiration in the writings of Donner, who used chess as a metaphor for his profound observations on art, culture and civilisation.' Keene is right, of course. Dutch grandmaster Hein Donner was an excellent writer and knew a lot, yet he really excelled as a conversationalist. It was a true pleasure to hear him tell a story. In the piece *What the Thunder Said*, Keene elaborates on an anecdote first described by Tim Krabbé. During the tournament of Venice 1967, Donner and American grandmaster Larry Evans are sitting on a terrace on San Marco Square, Donner expounding an interesting theory about the number of pillars on the square. Evans goes and counts the pillars, ascertaining that there is one fewer than the number Donner has based his theory on. 'Interesting but always wrong,' was his take on the great conversationalist.

I have always found this anecdote unsatisfactory, because it never said what the theory actually was. 'A magnificent lecture of cosmic proportions', Keene calls it. Larsen deflates this somewhat in his article 'Remembering Donner' for New In Chess 1989/3, writing: 'A wonderful story, something to do with the Napoleonic wars.' Interestingly enough, Keene talks about 37 pillars, whereas Larsen is going for 36. So were there 35 or 36 in reality? It should be possible to verify this. Meanwhile, we'll never know the true facts of the story.

Goethe's Faust
In his book, Keene always places chess in a wider perspective, especially a historical one. He speculates, for example, about the question of whether Conan Doyle saw Steinitz in Simpsons-in-the-Strand, posits a possible link between *Beowulf* and the Lewis chess pieces, and ponders the question of whether Shakespeare and Leonardo da Vinci played chess. It is not at all certain that Donner would have agreed with him on the two latter investigations. In 1965, he wrote about chess: 'The value of the game is not to be found in the fact that Goethe thought highly of it or that Jean Rostand played it – though badly. The game of chess is

Since 2014 Raymond Keene is also a Knight of the Order of the White Swan, conferred by Prince Marek Kasperski. No need to get nervous if you don't know the order or the prince.

a monument of culture because El Greco (*Il Calabrese*) played it, and Philidor, Lasker, Alekhine and Botvinnik. Because Nimzowitsch wrote about it, and Euwe. Because Troitzky abstracted beauty from it in his endgame studies.' Donner is quite right. Keene must know the passage as well, because it is to be found in *The King*. Yet he trots out Goethe in the piece entitled *The Touchstone of Intellect*, which is Goethe's characterization of chess. But then it turns out that Keene has a different purpose: he is a Goethe scholar and does not raise the subject of chess again. He investigates Goethe's influence on the music of Beethoven, Liszt and Mahler, with

He speculates about the question of whether Conan Doyle saw Steinitz in Simpsons-in-the-Strand

justified pride letting his readers know that he has translated *Faust* into English.

Civilising values
In his Introduction, Keene observes: 'Although this book contains a considerable amount of material which will primarily be of interest to the chess aficionado, I hope also that my thoughts will be of interest to those who see chess as an integral part of civilising values.' Chess as a springboard: this also features in the piece *Two Questions Posed by Borges*. Keene starts with a Borges quotation from 1981: 'Chess is one of the means to save culture, such as Latin, the study of the humanities, the reading of the classics, the laws of versification and ethics. Chess is now replaced by football, boxing or tennis, which are games of fools, not of intellectuals.' Borges said this in an interview, and after four decades his words have lost nothing of their relevance. Borges loved chess. In 1930, he wrote the poem *Chess*, and chess plays a part in three of his stories: *The Garden of Forking Paths*, *The Secret Miracle* and

Guayaquil. But this is not what Keene is talking about. He proffers a fascinating theory about Virgil, Augustus and the birth of Christ. He had told me about this 17 years ago, and it was a pleasant surprise to see it back in print and in greater detail.

Sometimes you're struck by a sense of melancholy in *Fifty Shades of Ray*. Keene retrieves a memory of Hastings 1973/74. After a gruelling game he repairs to the hotel bar to order a brandy. Then, Keene writes:

Keene's modest request was thwarted when he was told by the barman that Tal had consumed the hotel's entire stock of brandy

'My modest request was thwarted when I was told by the barman that "That Russian gentleman (he meant Tal) had consumed the hotel's entire stock of brandy during a drinking session into the early hours the night before".'

Monk-like existence
The contrast with modern-day top players couldn't be greater. About them, Keene writes: '... Modern elite grandmasters tend to follow a monk-like existence, based on the knowledge that smoking, drinking, and especially drugs are all utterly inimical to the fully functioning operation of the human brain.' Elsewhere, Keene describes the goings-on during the match between Steinitz and Chigorin in Havana 1892: 'The game was notable for the bracing refreshments selected by the masters during play. Chigorin was supplied with free brandy and Steinitz with unlimited champagne. Their glasses stood beside the board during play.

Steinitz explained later that he drank the champagne under medical advice in order to fortify his nerves.' Apparently, not only the top players but also the physicians of those days had different ideas about the effects of alcohol.

I don't always agree with Keene. I find his comparison between Fischer and Oedipus far-fetched. They are tragic for utterly different reasons. With whom could Fischer really be compared? One possibility is Grettir the Strong from the Icelandic sagas. Donner compared Fischer with someone from a more recent past. In 1976, he wrote: 'America is a country where people can behave more waywardly than anywhere else in the world, provided they have enough money. (...) In this, Bobby Fischer is reminiscent of the mysterious Howard Hughes, another hero of individualistic ideology'. And this was well before Fischer's tragic fate had fully played itself out.

In *Pyrenean Victory* Keene observes about Alekhine's infamous articles in the *Pariser Zeitung*: 'Quite possibly these clumsy articles were forgeries, as he (Alekhine) was later to claim.' I don't think there's any more doubt about this matter. Two decades ago, in Lisbon, I talked with Dagoberto Markl, author of *Xeque-mate no Estoril*. He showed me a copy of a handwritten article. I recognised Alekhine's handwriting. It was about Steinitz, whom it describes in very negative terms. 'And Steinitz was Jewish', Markl said.

Beating Botvinnik
Fifty shades of Ray contains many famous historical games, but also a considerable number of Keene's own. An example is the author's reminder to his readers that he defeated Botvinnik at age 18.

Raymond Keene
Mikhail Botvinnik
Hastings 1966/67 (3)
King's Indian Defence, Fianchetto Variation
1.♘f3 g6 2.c4 ♗g7 3.d4 ♘f6 4.g3

0-0 5.♗g2 c6 6.0-0 d6 7.♘c3 a6 8.a4 a5 9.b3 ♘a6 10.♗a3 ♘b4 11.e4 ♗g4 12.♕d2 ♗xf3 13.♗xf3 ♘d7 14.♖ab1 ♕b6 15.♖fd1 ♖ad8 16.♘e2 e5 17.♗g2 ♖fe8 18.d5 ♘c5 19.♘c1

19...♖f8
About this move Keene observes: 'Discrete, but powerful. Note that Black has the initiative on both sides of the board and that his pieces are indirectly all aiming at White's main weakness, the f2-square.' This is not implausible as a comment, but Keene is far too pessimistic about his own chances here. The computer sees an advantage for White! It's true that the black knights are blocking the queenside, but Black can't achieve anything concrete with this. White has not only more space, but also the bishop pair.
20.♗b2
Not a very purposeful move, handing the advantage to Black. Strong was 20.♘a2!, attacking the foothold on b4.

ANALYSIS DIAGRAM

A possible continuation is 20...♘ca6 21.♘xb4 ♘xb4 22.c5! ♕xc5 23.♗xb4 axb4 24.♖bc1 ♕b6 25.dxc6 bxc6

**Raymond Keene in action at the chessboard in the 1960s.
He received the GM title in 1976, at the same FIDE Congress where
Tony Miles, the first British grandmaster, was awarded the title.**

26.♕c2 c5 27.♗f1, and White has a clear positional advantage. Black's extra pawn carries no weight.

20...cxd5 21.cxd5 f5 22.exf5 gxf5 23.♖e1

The immediate 23.♗c3 would have been slightly better.

23...♖c8

A systematic move: Botvinnik occupies the open file. Far stronger, however, would have been 23...♖f6!, with the devastating threat of 24...♗h6. White has no worthwhile defence; 24.♔h1 is met by 24...♘e4, and wins.

24.♗c3 ♘e4

Not very effective here. With 24...e4, Black could have aimed for a bishop swap, with a positional advantage.

25.♗xe4 fxe4 26.♗xb4 ♗h6

Botvinnik had apparently overestimated this sequence. The resulting position is only good for a draw. This also goes for 26...axb4, incidentally. After 27.♖xe4 (Keene's 27.♖b2 is less good; after 27...e3! 28.♕xe3 ♕xe3 29.fxe3 e4 Black is better) 27...♗h6 28.♕e1! ♖xc1 29.♖xc1 ♗xc1 30.♖xb4 ♕a7 31.♕xc1 ♕xf2+ 32.♔h1 Black has nothing more than a draw.

27.♕xh6 ♕xf2+ 28.♔h1 ♕f3+ 29.♔g1 ♕f2+ 30.♔h1

30...♖c2

Botvinnik refuses to settle for a draw.

31.♕h3 ♕f3+ 32.♔g1 axb4

And he keeps trying.

33.♘e2 ♕e3+ 34.♔h1

34...♖xe2?? A terrible blunder. Botvinnik must have suffered a sudden lapse of concentration. After 34...♖f2 White would have had no more than a draw by repetition. After

'At which point Botvinnik gasped, raised his hand to his forehead and resigned'

34...♕f3+ 35.♕g2 e3 36.♕xf3 ♖xf3 37.♖bc1 ♖d2 the position would have been equal, too.

35.♕g4+ Keene writes: 'At which point Botvinnik gasped, raised his hand to his forehead and resigned.'

In the same tournament, Botvinnik also found himself in a losing position against Michael Basman, but managed to save the game in a long endgame. This leaves Keene as the only Englishman besides C.H.O'D. Alexander to beat Botvinnik. Alexander's victory in the famous Radio Match of 1946 was convincing, but Botvinnik managed to get his revenge 12 years later in the Munich Olympiad. He never got that chance against Keene, their Hastings game being the only one they ever played. ■

Raymond Keene, Fifty Shades of Ray, Chess in the year of the Coronavirus pandemic, Hardinge Simpole 2021, 302 pages

A place in the sun

If you haven't decided on your summer reading yet, **MATTHEW SADLER** has some tasty suggestions. From inspirational opening books to *The Unstoppable American*, Jan Timman's new page-turner on Bobby Fischer.

After a sustained period of grim weather, summer has suddenly remembered that it is still allowed to visit England (subject to new tougher Brexit rules). So I'm writing this while sitting in the sun in my parents' back garden! Following a period of work unparalleled in my career – I have never worked so many hours for such a long time, even when I was seconding Joel Lautier ☺ – it's a relief to get back to the essential business of reading chess books!

Looking at the books in front of me, I was a little worried that my wrecked brain might crash at the detail and complexity of the material, but in the end I only had to put Boris Gelfand's latest astonishingly detailed book aside for later study. All the rest I managed!

We start off with *1.e4!, The Chess Bible, Volume One* by the young Australian Grandmaster Justin Tan (Thinkers Publishing). This substantial 456-page book (the first of a planned series of three) covers White systems against five openings: the Alekhine, the Nimzowitsch (1.e4 ♘c6), the Scandinavian (1.e4 d5 2.exd5, 2...♘f6 and 2...♕xd5), the Pirc/Modern, and the Philidor. The material is well-structured, each section prefaced by an overview (summarising the key conclusions) and an explanation of the general concepts.

I would call this a very objective book. I mean this in the sense that the author chooses what he considers are the best lines against each opening, rather than looking for a common piece setup that can be applied – for better or for worse – against everything. For example Tan recommends the Four Pawns Attack against the Alekhine and investigates deeply the tactical refutation of the 2...♘f6 Scandinavian, but also recommends quiet ♗e2 systems against the Pirc and the Modern.

I spent some time working through the book and I was extremely impressed. I've read a lot of very good books on 1.e4 openings recently (both for the white and black sides) but this book still manages to add plenty of new material while consistently being spot on in its judgments even in the most unusual lines. For example, I was interested to read that Tan had analysed and then rejected 2.d4 as an answer to the Nimzowitsch (1.e4 ♘c6), as he could not find any clear advantage after 2...d5 3.e5 ♗f5. I share this seemingly odd conclusion and it is also borne out by recent top-level engine games, one of which I can't resist quickly sharing here:

Stockfish Classical
Leela Zero
TCEC Season 17 Superfinal 2020 (71.1)
1.e4 ♘c6 2.d4 d5 3.e5 ♗f5 4.c3 e6 5.♗e2 f6 6.f4 g5 7.♗h5+ ♚d7 8.fxg5 fxe5 9.♘f3 h6

10.g4 ♗e4 11.♘bd2 ♗xf3 12.♘xf3 e4 13.♘h4 hxg5 14.♘g6 ♖h7 15.0-0 ♗d6 16.♕e2 a6 17.♔g2 ♖g7 18.♗e3 ♘ge7 19.♘f8+ ♕xf8 20.♖xf8 ♖xf8 21.♖f1 ♗f4

22.h4 ♖h8 23.hxg5 ♗xg5 24.♗xg5 ♖xg5 25.♔f2 ♘f5

Justin Tan manages to add plenty of new material while consistently being spot on in its judgments even in the most unusual lines

26.♔e1 ♘ce7 27.♕f2 ♖hxh5
28.gxh5 ♖xh5 29.♔d1 ♖h4 30.a3
♘g6 31.♔c1 e3

With a wild game ending in a draw in 199(!) moves.

I also found the section on ♗e2 systems against the Pirc/Modern extremely refreshing and a welcome change from the normal recommendations of ♗e3 and f3 systems. In particular I liked very much the switch into King's Indian-type positions after 1.e4 d6 2.d4 ♘f6 3.♘c3 g6 4.♘f3 ♗g7 5.♗e2 0-0 6.0-0 a6 7.a4 ♘c6 8.a5 e5 9.d5 ♘e7 10.♘d2

when White may continue with ♘a4, c4 and c5.

In conclusion, a series that I am looking forward to seeing completed with plenty of inspiration and ideas for the serious 1.e4 player! Recommended, 4 stars!

■ ■ ■

Talking of inspiration, as an inveterate French player I was glad to see another cauldron of sizzling French ideas heading my way with *The Fully-Fledged French* by Viktor

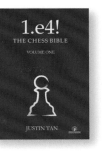

1.e4!
The Chess Bible
Volume One
Justin Tan
Thinkers Publishing,
2021
★★★★☆

Moskalenko (New In Chess). Every six or seven years, Moskalenko seems to come up with a grand tour of the French Defence (*The Flexible French* in 2008 and *The Even More Flexible French* in 2015 were the forerunners to this volume), in which he presents a series of new ideas in different variations, to freshen up your repertoire.

I have to declare an interest here as to my surprise one of my ideas gets heavily featured in Chapter 9:

Fabien Libiszewski
Matthew Sadler
England 2018
1.e4 e6 2.d4 d5 3.♘d2 ♗e7 4.♘gf3 ♘f6 5.e5 ♘fd7 6.♗d3 c5 7.c3 ♘c6 8.0-0 g5 9.dxc5 ♘dxe5 10.♘xe5 ♘xe5 11.♘b3 ♘xd3 12.♕xd3

And now the lovely idea **12...f6** of which I was indeed very proud! Moskalenko asks whether the idea was discovered by AlphaZero or by me, but I'm afraid that this one was all me ☺. The idea just flashed into my head after noticing that the immediate 12...e5 is irritatingly met by 13.♕e2 f6 (13...♗f6 14.♗xg5) 14.♕h5+ ♔f8 15.h4. I loved the flexibility of the structure immediately

The Fully-Fledged French
Viktor Moskalenko
New In Chess, 2021
★★★★☆

and it even turned out to be a strong idea!

13.f4 gxf4 14.♗xf4 e5 15.♗h6 ♖g8 16.♕xh7 ♗e6 17.♗g7 ♕d7 18.♔h1 ♘d8 19.♕g6+ ♗f7 20.♕g3 ♗e7 21.♘a5 b6 22.cxb6 axb6 23.♘b3 ♖a4 24.h3 ♖e4 25.a4 d4 26.cxd4 ♕d5 27.a5 ♕xb3 28.♕xb3 ♗xb3 29.dxe5 fxe5 30.axb6 ♖xg7 31.b7 ♗d6 32.♖a8+ ♔e7 0-1.

Moskalenko has a unique approach to presenting his ideas, dotting his analysis with key words such as WEAPON (indicating an interesting, untested idea), TRICK (watch out for the tactic!), PLAN and PUZZLE (move-order subtlety). The first time I came across this, it felt a little gimmicky, but I've grown

Moskalenko asks whether the idea was discovered by AlphaZero or by me, but I'm afraid that this one was all me ☺

to accept and even like it, as it helps keeps you alert while reading. All-in-all, another good book to the normal excellent standard we expect from Moskalenko! 4 stars!

■ ■ ■

I've been blessed with opening books this month, as I also greatly appreciated *The Italian Renaissance I and II* by Ukrainian grandmaster Martin

The Italian Renaissance I and II
Martyn Kravtsiv
Quality Chess, 2020
★★★★☆

Tactical Training
Cyrus Lakdawala
Everyman Chess, 2021
★★★☆☆

Kravtsiv (Quality Chess). Actually, the title really sells this 2-volume series short, as these two volumes also cover the Bishop's Opening (1.e4.e5 2.♗c4) – which often transposes to the Italian but which has many independent paths too –, the Petroff (1.e4 e5 2.♘f3 ♘f6), which is Black's main way to avoid the Italian Game, as well as the Italian Game itself: 1.e4 e5 2.♘f3 ♘f6 3.♗c4.

Again there have been many decent books recently on the Italian – *Winning with the Slow (but Venomous!) Italian* by Souleidis and Müller (New In Chess) and *The Modernized Italian Game for White* by Kalinin and Kalinichenko (Thinkers Publishing) to name just two – but this one is clearly my favourite. It's a real grandmaster repertoire – Kravtsiv doesn't shun extremely deep analysis of some critical middlegame positions – but there is a lot of grandmaster judgement in the lines too. Kravtsiv always has an eye for a position that his engines consider equal but that might be easier for White's game and I have to say that I agreed with a lot of his evaluations. Excellent work – 4 stars!

■ ■ ■

When the sun is beating down on you, and you're feeling a little tired and sleepy, you really appreciate an author who pulls you through training material in a chatty and entertaining fashion, and *Tactical Training* by Cyrus Lakdawala (Everyman) is just such a book! The premise of the book is the following: 'This is what this book attempts: to get you to shift your study focus to training in

tactics, combinations and calculation... Students show me their games and in the vast majority miss basic tactical opportunities in almost every game. The aperture of opportunity closes quickly. Miss your combination – or your opponent's combination against you – and we can easily flip a win into a draw or loss.' Having spent many hours during lockdown commentating on the games of amateur players, I completely agree with Lakdawala's assessment. The number of missed opportunities per game is significant; correcting this could make a huge difference to the players' ratings.

After an overview of basic mating themes, we go through several chapters of mates, moving progressively from short to long (the final puzzle is 50 moves!) After that we have a long series of thematically-organised chapters (Decoy/Attraction/Removal of the Guard, Discovered Attack, Overloaded Defender(s)). The final chapter is a look at the taken and missed opportunities in a recent Carlsen-Nakamura online match. As I said, I enjoyed browsing through this book in a relaxed manner and this is partly due to the light tone and to the

The number of missed opportunities in amateur games is significant; correcting this could make a huge difference to the players' ratings

nice mix of positions from real games and from composed studies.

There was plenty that made me go ooh and aah, such as this lovely little 1896 study by M. Lewitt:

M. Lewitt
1896

1.a5 h3 2.g4+ ♚h4 3.a3 h5

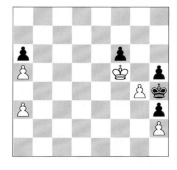

Wait for it! **4.g5 fxg5 5.a4 g4 6.♚f4 g3 7.hxg3** Mate.

I also loved this Bronstein gem, which I had somehow never seen before!

David Bronstein – Vladas Mikenas
Soviet Union 1941

22.♘b5+ cxb5 23.♕xb5 ♖e8 24.♖e7+ Beautiful! **24...♖xe7 25.♕c6** Mate.

A perfect summer holiday book for relaxing on a beach with a cool drink! 3 stars!

■ ■ ■

The Unstoppable American by Jan Timman (New In Chess) is – just like Jan's *The Longest Game: The Five Kasparov-Karpov Matches for the World Chess Championship* – a book that looks back at a famous episode in chess history from a modern perspective. *The Unstoppable American* chronicles Fischer's sensational run from the 1970 Palma da Mallorca Interzonal until the Candidates Final against Petrosian through 63 annotated games.

As a player who started my chess in the mid-1980s, I didn't experience the Fischer phenomenon. The knowledge I gained about him was the stuff of legends: he had demolished everyone in just two years, become World Champion and then left the game. That's a very evocative story, but actually much less interesting than the nuanced story which Timman details through anecdotes and analysis. The point is that this was a very difficult and strenuous path for Fischer. Apart from his own unpredictable doubts and demons, there were many difficult games in which half points had to be saved through frantic adjournment analysis, frustrating failures to overcome weaker players and unexpected periods of fragility. And yet what strikes you most as Timman takes you through each tournament game by game is the stability of Fischer's play: some-

times extremely powerful, sometimes less inspired but never less than completely focused whatever the stage of the game. That's an astonishing achievement over such a period of time against such strong opposition.

Timman's annotations are really good: generally not too variation heavy, full of human insight and strong in identifying the turning points of games. Looking at Fischer's games with the benefit of an engine, you see that he did – by engine standards – make numerous small inaccuracies while converting his advantages but you also understand what a fantastic feel Fischer had for the crucial moments in a game. You don't see many examples in his play of passivity or failing to take action when it was required. I thought that his game against Miguel Najdorf from the Siegen Olympiad 1970 was a good illustration of this.

Bobby Fischer
Miguel Najdorf
Siegen Olympiad 1970
Sicilian Defence, Kan Variation

1.e4 c5 2.♘f3 e6 3.d4 cxd4 4.♘xd4 a6 5.♗d3 ♘f6 6.0-0 d6 7.c4 ♗d7 8.♘c3 ♘c6 9.♗e3 ♗e7 10.h3 ♘e5 11.♗e2 ♖c8 12.♕b3 ♕c7 13.♖ac1 0-0 14.f4 ♘c6

15.♘f3 A strong move. White evades piece exchanges, to derive optimal profit from his spatial advantage.
15...♕b8 On 15...♘a5, White would have reacted with 16.♕d1, and Black cannot take the c-pawn. Now the knight sortie is threatened.

16.♕d1 Anticipating the sortie of the black knight.
16...♗e8 17.♕d2 ♘a5 18.b3 b6 19.♗d3 ♘c6 20.♕f2 b5 Finally Black has managed to make this traditional push. However, it doesn't bring him much relief.
21.♖fd1 ♘b4 22.♗f1 bxc4

23.bxc4 The correct recapture. White now controls the centre optimally, while the c-pawn doesn't become weak.
23...a5 24.♘d4 ♕a8

25.♕f3 Sharper was the pawn sacrifice 25.g4 which is in fact a pseudo-sacrifice. After 25.g4 ♘xe4 26.♘xe4 ♕xe4 27.a3 ♘a6 28.♗g2 ♕g6 29.♗b7 White wins the exchange.
25...♘a6 An excellent regrouping. The knight is on its way to c5.

Timman's annotations are not too variation heavy, full of human insight and strong in identifying the turning points of games

26.♘db5 ♘c5

27.e5 Fischer has seen sharply that his chances lie in the endgame; he will get a dominant knight on d6. Less strong was 27.♘xd6, since White hardly has any advantage after 27...♗xd6 28.♖xd6 ♘cxe4 29.♘xe4 ♘xe4 30.♖b6 ♗c6.

27...dxe5 28.♕xa8 ♖xa8 29.fxe5 ♘fe4

A better defence was 29...♘fd7, to block the white c-pawn as firmly as possible. Also in that case, White will post his knight on d6. There could follow

I imagine myself playing against Fischer's relentless logic and I'm not sure I like the outcome!

30.♘d6 f6 31.exf6 gxf6 32.♖b1 ♗g6 33.♖b5 ♖a6 34.♘b7 ♖c8 35.♘a4 and Black has no good way to maintain the blockade on c5. White has the advantage but Black can still fight.

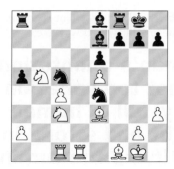

30.♘d6

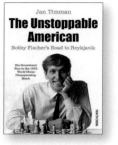

The Unstoppable American Jan Timman New In Chess, 2021
★★★★☆

A standard reaction; however, 30.♘xe4, to give the c-pawn free passage, would have been much stronger. Frankly, it's strange that Fischer didn't play this since the whole line can be concretely calculated. After 30...♘xe4 31.c5 ♗c6 32.♗d3 ♘g3 33.♘d4 ♗a4 34.♖e1 White is winning.

30...♗c6

This blockade of the c-pawn turns out to be insufficient. Black should have exchanged the knights and then regrouped: 30...♘xc3 31.♖xc3 and now he could have followed up with 31...♗a4 32.♖e1 ♘d7 33.♗d4 ♖fb8 when White has some advantage thanks to his strong knight, but Black has good piece coordination.

31.♘cxe4 ♘xe4 32.c5

And so White has managed to break through with his c-pawn after all. The remaining blockade on c6 is unstable.

32...♘g3 33.♗c4 h5 34.♗f2 h4 35.♗xg3 hxg3 36.♗b5

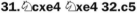

The blockade is broken.

36...♗xb5 37.♘xb5 f6 38.♖d7 ♗d8 39.♖c3 The easiest path to the win. **39...fxe5 40.♖xg3 ♖f7 41.♖xf7 ♔xf7 42.c6 ♗b6+ 43.♔f1 ♔f8 44.c7 ♖c8 45.a4 e4 46.♔e2 e5 47.♖g6 ♗d4 48.h4 ♗b2** Black resigned.

I really liked this game, which I had not seen before. There was the first acceleration around move 15, when Fischer regrouped his pieces strongly to secure a clear advantage, with some nice details like capturing on c4 with the b-pawn to maintain White's central control. Fischer's solid 25.♕f3 seemed designed to maintain White's advantage without complications. However, after Najdorf's nice regrouping 25...♘a6, Fischer sensed the right moment to change the situation and accelerate the play again. Fischer's execution idea was not engine-perfect but still totally logical. The chance Najdorf got would only have been the first step on a treacherous path to holding a draw! After Najdorf's plausible 30...♗c6, Black's position was just swept away. I imagine myself playing against such relentless logic and I'm not sure I like the outcome! Another really good book – we really are lucky to have such fine players and legends as Jan writing books like this! 4 stars! ∎

We really are lucky to have such fine players and legends as Jan writing books like this!

They are The Champions

**PATRICIA CASTILLO PENA
Dominican Republic**

Woman Candidate Master Patricia Castillo is the 2021 women's champion of the Dominican Republic. The country's national women's championship was an eight-round Swiss tournament held over two weekends in Santo Domingo in April. Patricia finished clear first with 6 ½ out of 8, ahead of the other 21 participants. In the first round, she won by forfeit when her opponent failed to show up.

Chess for Patricia is a serious hobby, and she loves to study the games of the great masters of the past and follow the top tournaments held around the world. Besides a chess player, Patricia is a coordinator of cultural events, and she is studying for her bachelor's in Industrial Psychology. During the opening ceremony of the tournament, the Minister of Higher Education, Science and Technology announced that the first-prize winners will be awarded university scholarships. Patricia will use this award to continue her education and obtain a master's degree in Strategic Management of Human Talent.

During the championship the Covid-19 situation in the country was challenging, with ICUs in hospitals close to full capacity and oxygen supplies running low, and the government had to announce additional lockdown measures to bring the infection rates down. The Covid-19 measures during the tournament included mandatory masks, social distancing, temperature checks and disinfection of hands, chess sets and the playing area.

Patricia Castillo is now a three-time National Champion and she has represented her country at the Chess Olympiad five times. At the 2018 Olympiad in Batumi, Georgia, she was awarded the title of Woman Candidate Master. This was one of Patricia's best chess experiences, meeting so many chess legends and friends in person. It was also her first trip abroad.

In 2017, Patricia played one of her best games in the National Women's Championship against Elizabeth Hazim Gonzalez.

Patricia Castillo Pena (1760)
Elizabeth Hazim Gonzalez (1819)
Santo Domingo 2017

position after 18...♗c6

White's a2-bishop seems out of play, looking at the pawn formation b5-c4-d5. Patricia reactivates her bishop via the b1-square and launches a crushing attack on Black's king. **19.♗b1 ♛b7 20.♗f5 ♘xf4 21.♗xf4 ♖fe8 22.♕g3 g6 23.e6 ♘f8 24.exf7+ ♖xf7 25.♘e5+ ♚g7 26.♗h6+ ♚g8 27.♗xg6 ♘xg6 28.♘xg6 ♗h4 29.♘e7++ 1-0.**
A model Sicilian Grand Prix attack!

In 2019, Patricia won the Women's Pan-American Amateur Chess Championship's Under-2000 category in Costa Rica, which qualified her for the Amateur World Championship to be held in Greece later this year. At said event, Patricia made a draw in the final round and returned to her hotel room disappointed, thinking that the draw would not be sufficient to win her category. Patricia did not even plan to attend the award ceremony, but then the organizers called her to inform her that the draw had been sufficient after all! She quickly had to get ready and jumped into an Uber taxi to arrive just in time to receive her first prize. Patricia felt incredibly happy!

Patricia lives by Einstein's quote, 'Genius is 1% talent and 99% hard work', and is preparing hard for the Amateur World Championship. She wants to increase her general level of play in order to obtain the WIM title. In the future, Patricia would like to have a chess school dedicated to developing female chess, where she will be able to promote chess and raise the level of the chess players in her country. ■

In **They are The Champions** we pay tribute to national champions across the globe. For suggestions please write to editors@newinchess.com.

Peter Wells

CURRENT ELO: 2397

DATE OF BIRTH: April 17, 1965

PLACE OF BIRTH: Portsmouth, UK

PLACE OF RESIDENCE: Swindon, UK

What is your favourite city?
Probably Edinburgh.

What drink brings a smile to your face?
Beer, especially with a hint of citrus fruit. I'm also a hopeless coffee addict.

Which book would you give to a friend?
Recently it has mostly been *Chess Improvement: It's all in the mindset* ☺.

What book are you currently reading?
Irrationality by Justin E. H. Smith. I don't agree with some of the conclusions, but the breadth of learning and the ambition is awesome.

What is your all-time favourite movie?
David Lean's *Doctor Zhivago*.

And your favourite TV series?
I am sceptical of hype, but *Breaking Bad* turned out to be as gripping as billed.

What music do you listen to?
Currently I am enraptured by George Enescu's 1st String Quartet.

What is your earliest chess memory?
I remember playing many games with my Dad, who advocated 'getting the queen out early to do a bit of damage'. Eventually, after losing much material, I guess I managed to defeat this strategy.

Who is your favourite chess player?
Mikhail Tal. More recently, I've been a huge fan of Vladimir Kramnik for the clarity of his play and his commentary.

Is there a chess book that had a profound influence on you?
I received Fischer's *My 60 Memorable Games* at a very young age and it would be hard to overestimate the initial impetus this gave me.

What was the best game you played?
Tough to pick, but I like my Greek gift against Dragos Nicolae Dumitrache at Balatonbereny 1997, since the follow-up was quite original.

What is your favourite square?
I would have said f5, but Luke McShane pointed out that I have had a good time sacrificing pieces on f4 as White, so perhaps I should adjust by a square.

Do chess players have typical shortcomings?
They are not always great at switching conversation topic in the presence of non-chess playing company.

Do you have any superstitions concerning chess?
Not really. This question should have been abandoned after Laurent Fressinet's answer 'I am not superstitious. It brings bad luck' – which is unsurpassable.

Facebook, Instagram, Snapchat, or?
I am on Facebook, but in name only. My only social media activity is on Twitter.

Who do you follow on Twitter?
Chess players (and chess historians), some philosophers and thinkers.

What is your life motto?
I don't really do mottos and if I did, I doubt they would survive a whole lifetime.

Who or what would you like to be if you weren't yourself?
Maybe an academic or journalist – certainly someone engaging with ideas.

Which three people would you like to invite for dinner?
Let's try Theodor Adorno, Hannah Arendt and Roger Scruton – that should be fairly lively.

What would people be surprised to know about you?
That I returned to university to get postgraduate degrees in my forties...

Where is your favourite place?
I love small islands where you can see the sea on all sides.

What is your greatest fear?
I am bad with heights. For the world, I am very concerned how intolerant we are becoming of diverse opinions – history suggests this tends to end badly.

How do you relax?
By playing the piano. But I am becoming corrupted by Netflix.

If you could change one thing in the chess world, what would it be?
I don't think I am overly conservative, but I am more worried that in 10 years' time there will be things I would like to change back to how they are now.

Is a knowledge of chess useful in everyday life?
Yes, particularly the thinking processes and mental toughness required for success at the game. We should also be good at decision-taking, but this does not appear to transfer so seamlessly.

What is the best thing that was ever said about chess?
I still like Tartakower's advice that 'every chess player should have a hobby'.